The Films of Fay Wray

The Films of Fay Wray

Roy Kinnard *and*
Tony Crnkovich

McFarland & Company, Inc., Publishers
Jefferson, North Carolina, and London

ALSO OF INTEREST AND FROM MCFARLAND

The Flash Gordon Serials, 1936–1940 (by Roy Kinnard, Tony Crnkovich and R.J. Vitone; 2008)

Science Fiction Serials: A Critical Filmography ... (by Roy Kinnard; 1998; paperback 2008)

Horror in Silent Films: A Filmography, 1896–1929 (by Roy Kinnard; 1995; paperback 1999)

"The Lost World" of Willis O'Brien: The Original Shooting Script ... (ed. by Roy Kinnard; 1993)

The present work is a reprint of the illustrated case bound edition of The Films of Fay Wray, *first published in 2005 by McFarland.*

Frontispiece: *portrait from* The Texan *(1930)*

LIBRARY OF CONGRESS CATALOGUING-IN-PUBLICATION DATA

Kinnard, Roy, 1952–
    The films of Fay Wray / Roy Kinnard and Tony Crnkovich.
      p.   cm.
    Includes bibliographical references and index.

    ISBN 978-0-7864-3875-4
    softcover : 50# alkaline paper ∞

    1. Wray, Fay, 1907–2004 — Catalogs. I. Crnkovich, Tony, 1962– II. Title.
PN2287.W74K56   2008
791.4302'8'092 — dc22   2005016985

British Library cataloguing data are available

©2005 Roy Kinnard and Tony Crnkovich. All rights reserved

No part of this book may be reproduced or transmitted in any form or by any means, electronic or mechanical, including photocopying or recording, or by any information storage and retrieval system, without permission in writing from the publisher.

On the cover: *Fay Wray*, a painting by Tony Crnkovich

Manufactured in the United States of America

McFarland & Company, Inc., Publishers
  Box 611, Jefferson, North Carolina 28640
  www.mcfarlandpub.com

To Fay Wray (1907–2004)
with sincere appreciation,
in remembrance of her
kindness and generosity

Acknowledgments

The authors would like to thank the following individuals, without whom this book would not have been possible.

First and foremost we thank, Fay Wray, who graciously consented to and took part in conversations and interviews regarding her career.

Direct quotes are taken from two interviews conducted by co-author Roy Kinnard, the first published in *Films In Review* in April 1990, the second in *Starlog* in September 1993. These quotes were approved by Miss Wray on original publication; her kindness, generosity and impressive memory are deeply appreciated by the authors.

The late George Turner and the late Edward L. Bernds also contributed information, as did Irving Lippman and Peter Schoedsack.

All photos herein are from the personal collection of co-author Tony Crnkovich. The cover illustration by Mr. Crnkovich is an *exact reproduction* of *King Kong* publicity photo #K-Adv-86, taken by RKO during production.

Contents

Acknowledgments vii
Introduction: The Queen of Screams 1

Part I. Silent Films 17
Part II. Sound Films 35
Part III. 1950s Feature Film Supporting Roles 163

Appendix I. Appearances in Theatrical Shorts 171
Appendix II. Television Appearances 175
Index 177

Introduction
The Queen of Screams

Fay Wray is best remembered today for her performances in *King Kong* and four other classic 1930s film thrillers (*Doctor X, The Most Dangerous Game, Mystery of the Wax Museum* and *The Vampire Bat*), but her film career encompassed much more than these memorable damsel-in-distress roles. She did not perform exclusively in the horror genre; only five of her 77 features from 1925 to 1958 (67 of them as a leading lady) can be classified as horror.

The extent of Wray's career, as documented in this book, may come as a surprise to many. A likable, dependable and competent actress, she has been directed by talents as diverse as William A. Wellman, Mauritz Stiller, Erich von Stroheim, Alan Crosland, Frank Capra, Raoul Walsh, Michael Curtiz, Jack Conway, Karl Freund, Roy William Neill and Josef von Sternberg. Her leading men have included Gary Cooper, Emil Jannings, William Powell, Richard Arlen, Jack Holt, Spencer Tracy, Ralph Bellamy, Fredric March, Wallace Beery, Joel McCrea, Claude Rains and Richard Barthelmess.

Five feet, three inches tall, with brown hair and blue eyes, Vina Fay Wray was born September 15, 1907, on her father's Alberta, Canada, farm. Her family moved to Los Angeles while she was very young. After performing in a few high school plays, Wray began working in movies at the age of 16 in 1923. Her first documented role was in a short subject called *Gasoline Love*; she went on to appear in comedy shorts for producer Hal Roach, mostly in bit parts with greats like Stan Laurel and Charley Chase. She made her feature film debut in *The Coast Patrol*, a low-budget independent production. A contract with Carl

Introduction: The Queen of Screams

This page: Late-1920s portrait (from *The Wedding March*). ***Opposite:*** Mid–1920s portrait, during her Western period at Universal Pictures

Laemmle's Universal Pictures followed; she was placed in a series of Westerns with cowboy stars like Art Acord, Jack Hoxie and Hoot Gibson.

It looked as though her career wouldn't advance beyond this point when she

Introduction: The Queen of Screams

landed the starring role in Erich von Stroheim's lavish production *The Wedding March*. She was only 18 at the time, but her performance as Mitzi in this tale of the ill-fated romance between a jaded aristocrat and a virginal commoner in old Vienna was of exceptional quality. Many of her scenes were touching, revealing an actress of dramatic range and emotional sensitivity. *The Wedding March* is certainly one of von Stroheim's finest pictures, both as director and actor, and Wray's showcase role should have made her a major star. It probably would have if the film hadn't taken so long to produce. By the time Paramount released the silent film in 1928, sound had already hooked the film-going public, and *The Wedding March* did not receive very wide distribution. Despite generally favorable reviews, relatively few people saw it. It was meant to be released in two feature-length parts, but the second half, *The Honeymoon* (now a lost film), was never released in the United States due to von Stroheim's objections over the final editing.

Wray did win a Paramount contract as a result of *The Wedding March*. Though most of the films she appeared in at that studio were innocuous and generally forgettable, there were a few noteworthy exceptions. She turned in a good performance in director Josef von Sternberg in *Thunderbolt*, and her supporting role in *The Four Feathers* introduced her to the producer-director team of Merian C. Cooper and Ernest B. Schoedsack, two iconoclastic filmmakers who would have bigger things in store for her with *King Kong*.

In 1928, Wray met writer John Monk Saunders (*Wings*) on the set of Paramount's *Legion of the Condemned*, in which she appeared with Gary Cooper. She and Saunders married later that same year. Wray's contract at Paramount had placed her in the front rank of movie stars in terms of salary and public visibility, but her tenure with the studio was not a long one. Decision-makers at Paramount attempted to pair her with Gary Cooper on several occasions, but the chemistry necessary for creating a box office team with wide appeal just wasn't there, and her films with Cooper generated only lukewarm audience response. Wray was released from her Paramount contract in 1931, and she then freelanced at a much lower salary. She appeared in *Dirigible* for director Frank Capra at Columbia, and in *Doctor X*, the first of her horror movie roles, for Warner Bros.-First National, looking especially attractive in the film's duo-tone Technicolor. *Doctor X* was soon followed by *The Most Dangerous Game* at RKO. The suspense thriller was directed by Ernest B. Schoedsack (with Irving Pichel) and produced by Merian C. Cooper, who was then preparing *King Kong*. Wray and her co-star in *The Most Dangerous Game*, Robert Armstrong, were assigned the leads in *Kong*, and the rest is film history. Wray's stature in Hollywood was somewhat dimin-

Introduction: The Queen of Screams

1930s studio portrait

ished by the termination of her Paramount contract, but *King Kong* gave her first billing in what would become one of the most popular and financially successful movies of the 1930s. She was suddenly in great demand, making an average

Introduction: The Queen of Screams

Fan magazine painting, early 1930s

Introduction: The Queen of Screams

1930s candid: Fay (*left*), with Lew Ayres, Ginger Rogers and Claudette Colbert.

of one film a month immediately after *Kong*. But this surge in popularity had little effect on the course of her career.

Although initially seen as little more than a popular, audience-pleasing "popcorn" movie, *King Kong*, with the passage of years and decades, through several reissues and then widespread television exposure, eventually became a classic and has been long considered a high watermark in special effects. Recent advances in computer-generated imagery have somewhat eclipsed older, hand-made films like *Kong*, but these same improvements in moviemaking technology have had another, unintended effect as well, throwing the film's other enjoyable qualities into sharper relief; the excellence of its visual design, its precise editing and its well-planned overall plot construction, all factors as vital to the movie's success as Max Steiner's throbbing music score. The cast, too, previously overshadowed in large part by the awe expressed over *Kong*'s special effects, can be more readily appreciated now; Fay Wray, in her ethereal, larger-than-life performance, is

Introduction: The Queen of Screams

1930s studio portrait

Introduction: The Queen of Screams

1930s fashion pose

one of the sweetest, sexiest heroines ever. She was then at the peak of her physical beauty, and her close-up in the film's mock "screen test" scene is one of the most attractive glamour close-ups ever shot in Hollywood.

Doctor X, The Most Dangerous Game, Mystery of the Wax Museum and *The Vam-*

Introduction: The Queen of Screams

Late 1920s candid, on the tennis court

pire Bat were all released around the same time as *King Kong*. The impression she made in these films is so indelible that it's easy to see why these particular movies have endured and still attract film buffs, overshadowing the rest of her career. Wray's

Introduction: The Queen of Screams

An eccentric studio portrait, 1920s

vulnerability, beauty and sex appeal were exploited to the hilt in these pictures. The first third of *King Kong* is virtually a showcase for her; In *Doctor X* and *Mystery of the Wax Museum* director Michael Curtiz seemed particularly aware of her

Introduction: The Queen of Screams

A 1930s studio portrait

sensuality. Wray made a determined effort to avoid horror films, though, perhaps out of awareness that she could easily become typecast in the genre. (Horror movie fans certainly would have appreciated seeing her in more of them.)

Introduction: The Queen of Screams

1930s Columbia Pictures portrait

She continued to work steadily at the major studios (she was in the prestigious *Viva Villa!* at MGM in 1934) until she traveled to Great Britain in 1935 to perform in a quartet of features there. Upon her return to Hollywood, her career

Introduction: The Queen of Screams

had lost momentum; though there was no shortage of work for her, from this point on she appeared almost exclusively in "B" pictures. Her contract with Columbia Pictures granted her the right to freelance elsewhere, and she did at RKO, Universal and Monogram. Few of the resultant films were noteworthy.

In 1939, she and John Monk Saunders, whose personal problems with drugs and alcohol had grown insurmountable, were divorced after the birth of their daughter Susan. Saunders committed suicide not long after the divorce. During this period, Wray had an affair with playwright Clifford Odets and a brief fling with tycoon Howard Hughes. Wray was now in her early thirties, with her film career on the downslide. She tried writing, collaborating with Sinclair Lewis on the play *Angela Is 21*, which was later filmed by Universal Pictures as *This Is the Life* (1944), starring Donald O'Connor and Susanna Foster; it was only marginally successful. Wray, who had starred in the Broadway plays *Nikki* and *The Brown Danube* in 1931, tried Broadway again a decade later in the plays *Golden Wings* and *Mr. Big*, but neither endeavor was a hit. After a few more "B" pictures at Columbia, she married Frank Capra's screenwriter Robert Riskin (the union produced two children, Victoria and Robert, Jr.), and retired from the screen at age 35. Her last film as a leading lady was Columbia's unremarkable *Not a Ladies' Man* (1942).

Her second marriage was a happy one, but Robert Riskin died tragically in 1955 from a brain embolism. Wray returned to movies in supporting roles, out of financial necessity as much as choice, and continued to work sporadically until 1958, after which she appeared in occasional guest roles on television through the mid–1960s. She officially retired in 1965, and in 1971 landed husband number three, prominent neurosurgeon Dr. Sanford F. Rothenberg (now deceased). She returned to acting one last time in support of Henry Fonda and John Houseman in the *Hallmark Hall of Fame* made-for-TV movie *Gideon's Trumpet* in 1980. More recently, she was reported to have been director James Cameron's initial choice for the role finally played by Gloria Stuart in the epic film *Titanic* (1998).

The true breadth of Fay Wray's film career is not readily apparent today, mainly because most of her films remain unavailable, for a variety of reasons. Some apparently do not exist in any form at all. With the fortunate exception of *The Wedding March*, virtually her entire silent output, including her co-starring films with Gary Cooper, is either lost or available on a limited archival basis. Interesting-sounding titles like RKO's gangster drama *The Big Brain* and the Karl Freund–directed Universal movies *The Countess of Monte Cristo* and *Madame Spy* are inaccessible as well. The result is that Wray is remembered now as a horror movie

Introduction: The Queen of Screams

actress, since those are her most frequently revived films. This is certainly not intended as a disparaging evaluation. The horror films that Wray appeared in are all classics, but she should have attained a more enduring stardom outside of that genre. The late director Edward L. Bernds, who began his career as a sound engineer at Columbia Pictures, speculated on why she never did in an interview with co-author Roy Kinnard: "She wasn't given the best of directors on her Columbia stuff—she could have been served better. Even a director like Roy William Neill [Wray's director on *Black Moon* and *Mills of the Gods*], who was capable of better work, didn't have the prestige at Columbia to make a film better in spite of everything. What she needed was a good, strong director with enough prestige to make a truly fine picture—maybe that's why she never went onward and upward." Bernds recalled her most vividly on the set of Capra's *Dirigible* in 1931. "She had all the good qualities. A beautiful girl, competent, thoroughly professional, and that, in my book, is high praise—to be professional." In his book *The Making of King Kong* (A. S. Barnes, 1975), the late co-author George E. Turner provided this cogent analysis of Fay Wray's appeal: "Never have the often contradictory qualities of sex appeal and virtue been blended more perfectly in one woman."

Living well into her nineties, Fay Wray was a reliable source of information on her movie career and Hollywood in general, both in interviews and in appearances at revivals of her films. One such memorable event held atop the Empire State Building was the 1989 book signing party to launch her autobiography *On the Other Hand*.

She passed away, quietly, in Manhattan on August 8, 2004. Fay Wray had often expressed fondness and respect for the New York landmark that contributed to her immortality. As an appropriate tribute to her enduring fame, on August 10, 2004, at 9:30 P.M., the Empire State Building's lights were dimmed for 15 minutes in honor of the beauty imperiled on its pinnacle 71 years before, and the charming actress who portrayed her.

The authors of *The Films of Fay Wray* present this book as a pictorial tribute to one of the horror film genre's most fondly remembered personalities—as well as one of Golden Age Hollywood's most beautiful and underrated actresses. The filmography is divided into three sections: first, Fay Wray's early silent feature film appearances; second, her "leading lady" period in the sound era; and third, her latter-day supporting roles. There are also two appendices; the first covers her appearances in theatrical film shorts, and the second her television appearances. All quotes from Wray are drawn from first-person, previously published interviews with co-author Roy Kinnard.

Part I
Silent Films

Note: When the exact running time of silent films is uncertain, the running time is given in the number of 35mm reels.

The Coast Patrol

Bud Barsky Corp., 1925; *Released:* March 20, 1925; *Director:* Bud Barsky; *Screenplay:* William E. Wing. Five reels (approximately 60 minutes).

Cast: Kenneth McDonald (Dale Ripley), Claire De Lorez (Valerie Toske), Fay Wray (Beth Slocum), Spottiswoode Aitken (Capt. Slocum), Gino Corrado (Eric Marmont).

Synopsis: Government revenue agent Dale Ripley pursues a ruthless gang of smugglers off the coast of Maine. Beth Slocum (FW), the innocent young daughter of elderly lighthouse keeper Capt. Slocum is misled by the gang's leader and is nearly victimized by him. With the aid of a former gang member, agent Ripley finally arrests the smugglers after their leader kills himself, winning Beth's love in the process.

Comments: This cheaply made feature from independent producer Bud Barsky was 17-year-old Fay Wray's feature film debut. The writer for the industry trade paper *Variety* (March 25, 1925) was critical of lead Kenneth McDonald but said that the movie compared "favorably with the better independent releases."

The Man in the Saddle

Universal, 1926; *Released:* July 11, 1926; *Producer:* Carl Laemmle, *Director:* Lynn Reynolds; *Story and Screenplay:* Charles A. Logue; *Photography:* Edwin (Eddie) Linden. Six reels (approximately 75 minutes).

Part I. Silent Films

The Coast Patrol

Cast: Hoot Gibson (Jeff Morgan, Jr.), Charles Mailes (Jeff Morgan, Sr.), Clark Comstock (Pete), Fay Wray (Pauline Stewart), Sally Long (Laura Mayhew), Emmett King (Tom Stewart), Lloyd Whitlock (Lawrence), Duke R. Lee (Snell),

Yorke Sherwood (Banker), William Dyer (Sheriff), Boris Karloff (Robber), Janet Gaynor (bit).

Synopsis: Tom Stewart, the owner of a ranch resort, is unknowingly victimized by Lawrence, his employee, who poses as a guide for visiting campers and then robs them. Heroic Jeff Morgan, Jr., the son of Stewart's friend, investigates and, at the urging of Stewart's daughter Pauline (FW), goes undercover as the leader of a camping party. After Lawrence and his gang are summoned by a flare signal from their accomplice Laura Mayhew, they hold up the campers. Jeff Morgan then tracks the band to their hideout, captures them and forces Lawrence to confess. With the mystery solved, Jeff becomes romantically involved with Pauline Stewart.

Mid–1920s Universal Pictures portrait

Comments: This bread-and-butter horse opera was Wray's first Western and her first picture under contract to Universal. Future stars Boris Karloff and Janet Gaynor (one of Wray's best friends in Hollywood) were at the bottom of the cast list in minor roles.

The Wild Horse Stampede

Universal, 1926; *Released:* September 5, 1926; *Producer:* Carl Laemmle; *Director:* Albert Rogell; *Screenplay:* Doris Malloy; Based on the story *Blind Trails* by W. C. Tuttle; *Photography:* William Nobles. Five reels (approximately 60 minutes).

Cast: Jack Hoxie (Jack Tanner), Fay Wray (Jessie Hayden), William Steele (Charlie Champion), Marin Sais (Grace Connor), Clark Comstock (Cross Hayden), Jack Pratt, George Kesterson, Bert De Marc, Monte Montague (Henchmen), Scout (Horse), Bunk (Dog).

Synopsis: Aided by his loyal horse and dog, Jack Tanner, a young rancher, corrals a herd of wild horses that have been ruining the local cattle ranges. Although he is romantically involved with Jessie Hayden (FW), Tanner is misled by a mysterious woman who turns out to be the wife of Charlie Champion, Tanner's rival. Jessie rejects Tanner when she sees him with Champion's wife, and their relationship is nearly ruined. The devious Champion's gang frees the wild horses in an attempt to steal them; the horses stampede and Champion is killed when he falls out of a wagon. Tanner rescues Jessie from the stampede, and they are reunited.

Comments: Another standard Universal Western, this oater played for only one day at the Tivoli theatre in New York (November 24, 1926). *Variety*, reviewing the film on December 1, found the picture fast-paced, commenting that the "stampede camera shots are okay, but produce nothing in the way of an innovation."

Lazy Lightning

Universal, 1926; *Released:* December 12, 1926; *Producer:* Carl Laemmle; *Director:* William Wyler; *Story and Screenplay:* Harrison Jacobs; *Photography:* Eddie Linden. Five reels (approximately 60 minutes).

Cast: Art Acord (Rance Lighton), Fay Wray (Lila Rogers), Bobby Gordon (Dickie Rogers), Vin Moore (Sheriff Dan Boyd), Arthur Morrison (Henry S. Rogers), George K. French (Dr. Hull), Rex De Roselli (William Harvey), Janet Gaynor (Bit).

Synopsis: Shiftless wanderer Rance Lighton (nicknamed "Lazy Lightning") is arrested for vagrancy and put to work on the Rogers Ranch. Dickie Rogers, a young invalid confined to a wheelchair, develops an affinity for Lighton. Henry Rogers, Dickie's uncle and heir to Dickie's share of the estate, conspires with his ruthless creditor, Bill Harvey, to dispose of Dickie. Becoming aware of this, Lighton opposes the villainous pair, saving Dickie's life and earning the devotion of the boy's sister Lila (FW).

Comments: William Wyler, later a major director, was related to Carl Laemmle, president of Universal, and was in the formative stages of his career at this point. *Variety*, reviewing the film on December 29, 1926, dryly noted that "there are some efforts to whip comedy into the film. Much of it lands with a thud."

Loco Luck

Universal, 1927; *Released:* January 23, 1927; *Producer:* Carl Laemmle; *Director:* Cliff Smith; *Screenplay:* Doris Malloy; Based on the story *The Eyes Win* by Alvin

J. Neitz; *Adaptation:* Isadore Bernstein; *Photography:* Eddie Linden; Five reels (approximately 60 minutes).

Cast: Art Acord (Bud Harris), Fay Wray (Molly Vernon), Aggie Herring (Mrs. Vernon), William A. Steele (Frank Lambert), Al Jennings (Jesse Turner, "Bush"), George F. Marion ("Dad" Perkins, Postmaster), M. E. Stinson (Mark Randell), George Grandee (George Kesterson), Art Mix.

Synopsis: Unscrupulous financier Jesse Turner moves to foreclose on the Vernon Ranch when he learns of an undiscovered oil deposit on the property. Bud Harris, a cowboy in love with Molly Vernon (FW), daughter of the ranch owner, enters a horse race so that he can pay the debt on the Vernon Ranch with the prize money. Turner kidnaps Bud, locking him in a remote cabin, but Bud is trailed and rescued by his horse. Bud manages to escape, arrive in time for the race and win the competition. With Turner's duplicity exposed, the oil deposit is discovered by the Vernons and Bud continues his romance with Molly.

Comments: Fay Wray was frustrated by her admittedly unimpressive career at Universal, which continued in the same vein with this predictable Western.

A One Man Game

Universal, 1927; *Released:* January 30, 1927; *Producer:* Carl Laemmle; *Director:* Ernest Laemmle; *Story and Screenplay:* William Lester; *Photography:* Harry Mason, Al Jones; *Art Director:* David S. Garber. Five reels (approximately 60 minutes).

Cast: Fred Humes (Fred Hunter), Fay Wray (Roberts), Harry Todd (Sam Baker), Clarence Geldert (Jake Robbins), Norbert Myles (Stephen Laban), Lotus Thompson (Millicent Delacey), William Malan (John Starke), Julia Griffith (Mrs. Delacey), Bud Osborne.

Synopsis: Fred Hunter and Jake Robbins prevent unscrupulous rancher Stephen Laban from coercing an unsecured loan out of the local bank. When Millicent DeLacey, an ambitious East Coast society girl, arrives in town, Fred Hunter poses as the "Duke of Black Butte," a nobleman, to impress her. Laban, who has been planning revenge, kidnaps Hunter, robbing the bank with his gang as a posse searches for Hunter. Roberts (FW), the tomboy daughter of Hunter's friend, discovers Hunter and releases him. After the bank robbers are arrested, Hunter admits that he loves Roberts, and they become romantically involved.

Comments: A One Man Game was released only three days after Wray's previous western *Loco Luck* (above). *Variety*, in a December 29 review, found the movie a "familiar type of western picture with a simple, obvious story to carry along the wild riding and fine scenic background."

Spurs and Saddles

Universal, 1927; *Released:* July 17, 1927; *Producer:* Carl Laemmle; *Director:* Clifford S. Smith; *Adaptation and Screenplay:* Harrison Jacobs; *Story:* Paul M. Bryan; *Photography:* Eddie Linden; *Art Director:* David S. Garber. Five reels (approximately 60 minutes).

Cast: Art Acord (Jack Marley), Fay Wray (Mildred Orth), Bill Dyer (Bud Bailey), J. Gordon Russell ("Blaze" Holton), C. E. Anderson ("Hawk"), Monte Montague (Stage Driver), Raven (Horse).

Synopsis: Adventurer Jack Marley, delivering a mailbag for a wounded Pony Express rider, stops a runaway stagecoach bound for the town of Caspar and falls in love with grateful passenger Mildred Orth (FW). Mildred has come west searching for her father, whom she has not seen since childhood. "Hawk" Kent, the crooked owner of the Caspar dance hall, becomes infatuated with Mildred and orders his lackey "Blaze" Holton to frame her, forcing her to work in the dance hall. Marley, aided by a guilty Holton, helps Mildred to escape. Before dying, Holton tells Mildred that she is heir to his money, admitting that he is really her father.

Comments: This film was Wray's last Universal Western after her contract was terminated by mutual consent and she left the studio to perform in director Erich von Stroheim's *The Wedding March*.

The Legion of the Condemned

Paramount, 1928; *Released:* March 10, 1928; *Producers:* Adolph Zukor, Jesse L. Lasky; *Director:* William A. Wellman; *Screenplay:* John Monk Saunders, Jean Di Limur; *Titles:* George Marion; *Photography:* Henry Gerrard; *Film Editor:* Alyson Shaffer. 74 minutes.

Cast: Gary Cooper (Gale Price), Fay Wray (Christine Charteris), Barry Norton (Byron Dashwood), Lane Chandler (Charles Holabird), Francis McDonald (Gonzolo Vasquez), Voya George (Robert Montagnal), Freeman Wood (Richard DeWitt), E. H. Calvert (Commandant), Albert Conti (Von Hohendorff), Charlot Bird (Celeste), Toto Guette (Mechanic).

Synopsis: During World War I, Gale Price joins the French Air Legion in

Part I. Silent Films

Legion of the Condemned: With Gary Cooper

disillusionment after he catches his girlfriend Christine Charteris (FW) dallying with a German officer. He later learns that she is actually an Allied spy when he is ordered to plant her behind German lines. The reunited lovers are captured by the Germans, but are eventually rescued by Price's unit.

Comments: Wray was cast as a French spy in love with Gary Cooper in this World War I drama, her first movie under her new Paramount contract. Wray's footage was not extensive; a new contractee, she was shoehorned into the cast, which was noted by the *Variety* reviewer who commented on the disparity between Wray's featured billing and her relatively few scenes. Scenarist John Monk Saunders took advantage of his assignment and got to know Wray better; they were married soon afterwards. Many stock shots of airplane dogfights from the same studio's previous hit *Wings*, also written by Saunders, were used to good advantage. *The Legion of the Condemned* was also Wray's first co-starring film with Gary Cooper. Despite Cooper's well-known reputation as a ladies' man, Wray insisted to co-author Kinnard (and reiterates in her autobiography *On the Other Hand*) that there was never any romantic involvement between them.

Part I. Silent Films

Legion of the Condemned: With Gary Cooper

Part I. Silent Films

The Street of Sin

Paramount, 1928; *Released:* May 26, 1928; *Producers:* Adolph Zukor, Jesse L. Lasky; *Associate Producers:* B. P. Schulberg, Benjamin Glazer; *Director:* Mauritz Stiller; *Screenplay:* Chandler Sprague; *Story:* Josef von Sternberg, Benjamin Glazer; *Titles:* Julian Johnson; *Photography:* Bert Glennon; *Set Design:* Hans Dreier, Edgar G. Ulmer; *Film Editor:* George Nichols, Jr. Seven reels (62 minutes).

Cast: Emil Jannings ("Basher Bill"), Fay Wray (Elizabeth), Olga Baclanova (Annie), Ernest W. Johnson (Mr. Smith), George Kotsonaros ("Iron Mike"), John Gough, Johnnie Morris (Cronies of "Basher Bill"), John Burdette (Proprietor of Pub).

Synopsis: Crooked prizefighter Basher Bill, falls in love with Elizabeth (FW), a Salvation Army girl. Influenced by her piety, Bill tells her about a bank robbery he has committed, vowing to go straight. Annie, a prostitute whom Bill had been involved with, is jealous and turns him in to the police. Then, feeling guilty, she warns Bill. The police capture Bill, who then sacrifices his life to save Elizabeth and the Salvation Army nursery when his former gang holds them hostage as they attempt to escape from the police.

Comments: Wray, only 20 years old, was in heady company with the great German actor Emil Jannings (her co-star) and prestigious director Mauritz Stiller, who had brought Greta Garbo to Hollywood. Wray recalled in her autobiography that she had originally been given a dramatic death scene in the film, but Jannings, who had the star power to demand script changes, had it re-written as *his* death scene. Bert Glennon is credited as photographer, but other (unverified) sources indicate that Harry Fischbeck and Victor Milner shot the film.

The First Kiss

Paramount, 1928; *Released:* August 25, 1928; *Producers:* Adolph Zukor, Jesse L. Lasky; *Director:* Rowland V. Lee; *Screenplay:* John Farrow; Based on the *Saturday Evening Post* story *Four Brothers* by Tristram Tupper; *Titles:* Tom Reed; *Photography:* Alfred Gilks. Six reels (approximately 61 minutes).

Cast: Fay Wray (Anna Lee), Gary Cooper (Mulligan Talbot), Lane Chandler (William Talbot), Leslie Fenton (Carol Talbot), Paul Fix (Ezra Talbot), Malcolm Williams ("Pap"), Monroe Owsley (Other Suitor).

Synopsis: In a desperate effort to restore his formerly respected but now poverty-stricken family's reputation, Mulligan Talbot becomes a pirate, robbing ships in Chesapeake Bay to finance his three brothers' educations.

Part I. Silent Films

***Street of Sin*:** With director Mauritz Stiller (*left*) and star Emil Jannings

After six years, Mulligan has accumulated great wealth, his brothers have become successful and respected, and he decides to repay the people from whom he had stolen, an act of contrition that results in his arrest. Anna Lee (FW), a wealthy local girl who had previously considered Mulligan unworthy of her affections, testifies on his behalf, as do his three brothers. He is found guilty, but paroled in Anna's care.

Comments: Wray received first billing in this modest film, which *Variety* found "a nice program picture…Fay Wray successfully records a certain winsomeness as the wealthy heroine" (Aug. 22, 1928). Director Rowland V. Lee, a somewhat stodgy but reliable craftsman, is best remembered today as the director of Universal's *Son of Frankenstein* and *Tower of London*, Boris Karloff vehicles from 1939.

The Wedding March

Paramount, 1928; *Released:* October 6, 1928; *Producers:* Adolph Zukor, Jesse L. Lasky; *Producer:* P. A. Powers; *Director:* Erich von Stroheim; *Screenplay:* Erich von

Stroheim, Harry Carr; *Photography* (black & white with Technicolor inserts): Hal Mohr, Buster Sorenson, Ben Reynolds; *Art Director:* Richard Day, Erich von Stroheim; *Original Music Synchronization:* J. S. Zamecnik; Song "Paradise" by Harry D. Kerr, J. S. Zamecnik; *Costumes:* Max Ree; *Assistant Directors:* Eddie Sowders, Louis Germonprez; *Second Assistant Directors:* Eddie Malone, Art Jell; *Military Consultants:* Count Albert Conti and D. R. O. Hatswell, R. N.; *Special Historical Consultant:* Archduke Leopold of Hapsburg. 115 minutes.

Cast: George Fawcett (Prince von Wilderliebe-Rauffenberg), Maude George (Princess von Wilderliebe-Rauffenberg), Erich von Stroheim (Prince Nicki), George Nichols (Fortunat Schweisser), ZaSu Pitts (Cecilia Schweisser), Hughie Mack (Wine Garden Proprietor), Matthew Betz (Schani Eberle), Cesare Gravina (Martin Schrammell), Dale Fuller (Mrs. Schrammell), Fay Wray (Mitzi Schrammell), Sidney Bracey (Navratil), Anton Vaverka (Franz Joseph I). Danny Hoy (Mountain Guide), Don Ryan (H. I. H. Leopold Salvator), Captain Peter von Hartmann, Carey Harrison, Schumann-Heink, Harry Reinhardt, Wilhelm von Brincken, Captain John S. Peters.

Synopsis: Vienna, 1914: Mitzi Schrammell (FW), a crippled harpist working at a wine garden, is romanced by jaded aristocrat Prince Nicki. Mitzi gradually falls in love with him, but, unknown to her, the Prince has been informed by his family that he must wed Cecilia Schweisser, the daughter of a wealthy commoner, for financial reasons.

Infuriated by Mitzi's love for Nicki, Schani Eberle, a jealous butcher, threatens to kill the Prince at his wedding to Cecilia, but Mitzi prevents the murder. As Prince Nicki leaves the church with his bride, he sees Mitzi — his true love — standing in the rain with the crowd watching the wedding procession, and gazes at her sadly, for the last time, as he drives away with Cecilia.

Comments: Erich von Stroheim's *The Wedding March* was that troubled director's seventh film, and arguably his best. *Greed* (1924) may be his most powerful work, but *The Wedding March* is surely his most romantic directorial effort and contains his most sensitive performance. This emotional story of ill-fated love between a Viennese nobleman and an innocent peasant girl began shooting in June of 1926, on a series of 36 meticulously detailed sets.

After an intensive nine months of shooting, the original $300,000 budget had soared to $1,250,000, and production was halted by producer P. A. "Pat" Powers. In an effort to recoup the considerable investment, and also to reduce the film's running time to a manageable commercial length, two separate features were culled from the enormous amount of footage shot, much against Erich von

Stroheim's wishes. The two features were *The Wedding March*, running 115 minutes, and *The Honeymoon*, a 70-minute feature that began by recapping the plot of *The Wedding March*, much in the manner of a serial chapter, and then continued the story. Prepared for South American and European distribution only, *The Honeymoon* no longer exists, but fortunately, the plotline of *The Wedding March* does reach a logical conclusion of sorts, enabling the film to stand alone as a self-contained work.

Director von Stroheim cast Fay Wray, then only 18 and still under contract to Universal. In her, von Stroheim saw a gentle, honest emotional quality that is apparent, in varying degrees, in all of her film work. It was von Stroheim, though, who brought her unique qualities to the surface as no other director ever would, and it was in response to his understanding guidance that she gave what remains her finest performance.

Wray recalled *The Wedding March* in detail for co-author Kinnard in an August 21, 1988 interview: "King Kong is my friend. He's been my public relations man for years. It was an extraordinarily good role, but the richness of the role that I had in *The Wedding March* appealed to me more, and that's very understandable, I think, since there weren't many nuances in the *King Kong* role. That was a fantasy, and there was a broadness to it that seemed unreal.

"I was at Universal Studios, under contract there, doing Westerns. It was a wonderful training experience, but I didn't feel that it was the ultimate, by any means. I had met a lady who was an agent for writers who came to the studio one day, and remembered me (we had met when doing errands one day). She stopped and told me about the film that von Stroheim was going to make, and I suppose I'd heard of it too. She said, 'You know, I think you'd be wonderful for it. Would you like to go see him?,' and I said, 'Of course, my goodness!' He was, to my mind, the most exciting director there was in Hollywood. But it never occurred to me that I was under contract to Universal. That never crossed my mind, I was so eager to have the opportunity to be considered for that film. So we made arrangements to go to the studio, and we went to have a meeting with the president of the organization which had been formed just to make *The Wedding March*.

"He was a Frenchman, and when he saw me he said, 'Oh no, you would not do, you just would not do! Von Stroheim is not tall, I think you are too tall, von Stroheim is brunette, he would need a blonde, it is impossible, no?' I just knew in my heart and soul that that part was going to be mine, and I could not take 'no' from him. I realized that I had on high heels for one thing, and that although I

Part I. Silent Films

The Wedding March: With Eric von Stroheim

very often wore my hair down in curls, on this occasion I had built it up very high on top, to look more grown up, the way a leading lady should. I said, 'Let me come back tomorrow, and I will look different,' and I was thinking, 'He must say yes, he must say yes,' and he said, 'Well, yes, yes, come back tomorrow.' … I just put on flat shoes and let my hair down. I went back with the lady agent the next day and he showed us the way to the little bungalow where von Stroheim's office was.

Part I. Silent Films

The Wedding March

"It was a very hot day. There was no air conditioning at that time. I say that because he was dressed in the most casual way. He was wearing a beautiful white linen shirt, with a very cut-down neck, and no sleeves at all, but he looked elegant at the same time. He asked us to come in and sit down across the desk from him, the agent at the far end of the desk. Von Stroheim began to talk, to tell the story of *The Wedding March*. He appeared to be talking to the agent, but he kept looking at me out of the corner of his eye to see how this was affecting me. He paced up and down, too, and he would stop in front of me and look at me. Suddenly he offered his hand to me. I stood up and he said, 'Goodbye, Mitzi,' and that was it, as though he had already decided. How simple, how beautiful. I was very much affected and I burst into tears. He found that very exciting, I think, and he said to the agent 'Oh, I can work with her, I can work with her!,' then he said, 'Let's go se Mr. [Emil] Offeman [the company president]'. They left me there in the office. I don't remember anything after that. I just sat there realizing that a perfectly wonderful thing had happened.

"During the time that he had been talking and watching me, he saw some-

The Wedding March songsheet cover

thing in me that he liked, and I certainly saw something in him that I felt so in tune with, and it was as if something was sealed between us, it was quite remarkable. Also, I think it was very interesting that he did recognize what he called a spiritual quality, because I've always felt that about myself, and I've never been a church person. I find that just an element of understanding that makes me feel good, that doesn't require going into any kind of organized religion whatsoever. I don't set myself up as any special person. I guess I'm an appreciator. I appreciate life, and I appreciate so many things, that that's sort of my heartbeat. That was lovely, that was a lovely first meeting, absolutely marvelous…

"But then, I had to get out of my contract at Universal. Mr. Offeman said it was up to me to do that, that they could not ask Universal to loan me, because they'd want too much money. 'It's up to you,' he said, 'even if you have to lie.' On the way home, I knew what I was going to do. I was certainly not going to lie, because this was too beautiful a moment to mess up with lies, and I knew there was someone at the studio, a casting director there who I felt I could really go and talk to, and tell him openly just what had happened, and that he would know and understand. And, you know, he *did*? That was marvelous. So then he took the responsibility of telling Mr. Laemmle that he thought they should really let me go. Not for *The Wedding March*—just let me go! They were not developing me very much, and it seemed best not to keep me under contract. Wasn't that wonderful? It was just simply the most wonderful thing that he did. I don't know who else in the world would have done that at that time. I went with him to meet Mr. Laemmle. I'd never met Mr. Laemmle except on that occasion. The man's name was Paul Kohner, and he became a terrific agent. He knew von Stroheim and cared a lot about him, and he had good feelings about me. He felt that it was the right thing to do, to make it as simple as possible for me and the whole situation. So that is really unforgettable, just unforgettable.

"The shooting of *The Wedding March* went so well! There were times that were difficult, and I understood that, I understood him instinctively. I knew that whatever he wanted to do, if he wanted to be wild and difficult, then that was what he would do. The first scene that we did together had to be done at night. Towards the morning, when the sun was rising, we rushed to finish because the light was spoiling the night effect. Of course we had the dialogue that von Stroheim had written, and even though it was a silent film the dialogue had to be just right and letter perfect. He forgot his lines and I was able, because I felt so much in the scene and was relating to him, to throw him cues that didn't spoil the scene, we kept going. Well, he was astonished, he was just so astonished that

I could do that, and then excited, very excited, so there was a rapport between us that was wonderful.

"Sometimes he'd get a little unreasonable and want me to cry, even in rehearsal. I thought that was unfair. I learned how to cry on that film, I think. But there were a lot of lovely moments, and they all seemed so real, everything was so real. I never felt there was any acting going on. When I took the string off the box of candy, von Stroheim said, 'When you do that, put it around your neck like you're saving it,' and I thought that was a brilliant little thing to do, because if she's a peasant girl she would think of that, and would save the string, every bit of it would be important to her. That was a sweet scene.

"There were some wonderful things in the second part, *The Honeymoon*. There were scenes that we shot high up in the Sierras and then we went back to the studio where they built a set to look like mountain scenery for closer shots. That was where we did our farewell scene. [My character] was going to return home to Vienna, and von Stroheim was to say goodbye to me. That really turned out to be goodbye between Erich von Stroheim and Fay Wray. At that point I didn't know, and maybe he didn't know either, that they were going to shut production down, because it was over budget, and there was an enormous amount of film to be cut, so that was truly our farewell scene.

"I didn't see von Stroheim again until several years later when he was playing in a stage version of *Arsenic and Old Lace*. I did not go to see the play, but a friend who was in the cast told me that von Stroheim hoped I would come to see him between scenes at a matinee. I went to his dressing room and he had this beautiful French girl [Denise Vernac] with him who was his companion for about 18 years. That meeting seemed fairly unreal. I was glad to see him again, and I'm sure he was glad to see me, or he wouldn't have asked that I come. But the meeting didn't have much animation, it was just kind of matter-of-fact. I didn't know how to shape it into anything else, particularly, and we just pretty much sort of stared at each other. The French girl stared at me and I stared at her. Von Stroheim and I said we were happy to see each other. Cliché things. I saw him one time after that, when he came to Hollywood and Willie Wyler gave a dinner party. Then, only a few years ago, someone came to see me here, at von Stroheim's request. I thought this was extraordinary. Not too long before von Stroheim had died, this man had been his friend. When he came, I thought surely if he came to talk about von Stroheim it was because he wanted to write down my memories of von Stroheim. And so we talked on that basis for awhile, and then, just before he was to go I said, 'Will you be writing this, will you be writing about von Stroheim?' He said, 'Oh, no, no, [and told me that von Stroheim once said to *him*,] If you ever go to the United States, will you please go to see her.' And I was absolutely choked up as I said goodbye to him. I was very touched by that, very touched that he would ask this man to come and see me. He didn't give him any particular message for me so it was a sweet and lovely gesture on his part, like a message of wonderful good feeling to me. I took it that way and I have to take it that way. It was beautiful, just beautiful.

"I saw at least one of his lesser films on television in which he acted, and I thought, he is the only thing I'm seeing this picture for or care about, and I'm sure that was true of the average viewer, because he's so compelling. I remember in *Sunset Blvd.* when he was playing the servant to Gloria Swanson, there was a scene where she was performing and he wanted her to be so good that you could see that in him, that he was giving her all her strength. He didn't say a thing, as I remember, but he watched her with that wonderfully supportive look.

"To have had *The Wedding March* for my first important film was extraordinary. If I could have gone on and done two or three or four pictures with von Stroheim, it would have made a very different kind of career for me. I would like to have had that happen but, failing that, I think it was beautiful to have had that opportunity at that point in my life. To be appreciated by von Stroheim was marvelous. None of the quality I had in *The Wedding March* and none of the freedoms that were allowed me in *The Wedding March* ever came my way again.

"There was so much tragedy around von Stroheim. There had been so much tragedy. And he was always looked upon, by many I think, as a self-indulgent, difficult director. Many people admired his work and many people criticized him, and those who did that, I think, would have been lucky to have had some of his talent, because I certainly recognized it, and I never again worked with anyone who could touch that. I admired him. I really admired him."

In its review of *The Wedding March* (Oct. 17, 1928), *Variety* said, "Miss Wray appeals and convinces as the shy, pretty-faced and innocent victim, while von Stroheim's scoundrel is again interesting, despite the half-hearted attempt to soften the character."

As for *The Honeymoon*, it is apparently lost beyond reclamation. The last surviving print, held by a European archive, was inadvertently destroyed decades ago, before preservation copies could be made. The production credits and cast listed here apply to that film as well.

Part II
Sound Films

The Four Feathers

Paramount, 1929; *Released:* June 12, 1929; *Associate Producer:* David O. Selznick; *Directors:* Merian C. Cooper, Ernest B. Schoedsack, Lothar Mendes; *Screenplay:* Howard Estabrook, Based on the Novel *The Four Feathers* by Alfred Edward Woodley Mason; *Adaptation:* Hope Loring; *Titles:* John Farrow, Julian Johnson; *Photography:* Robert Kurrie, Merian C. Cooper, Ernest B. Schoedsack; *Assistant Cameraman:* Cliff Shirpser; *Film Editor:* Ernest B. Schoedsack; *Music Score:* William Frederick Peters; *Assistant Director:* Ivan Thomas (81 minutes)

Cast: Richard Arlen (Harry Feversham), Fay Wray (Ethne Eustace), Clive Brook (Lt. Durrance), William Powell (Capt. Trench), Theodore von Eltz (Lt. Castleton), Noah Beery (Slave Trader), Zack Williams (Idris), Noble Johnson (Ahmed), Harold Hightower (Ali), Philipe De Lacy (Harry Feversham, age ten), E. J. Radcliffe (Col. Eustace), George Fawcett (Col. Faversham), Augustin Symonds (Col. Sutch), Rex Ingram (native)

Synopsis: British officer Harry Faversham leaves the service when called to duty in the Sudan, choosing to marry Ethne Eustace (FW) instead of going to war. Three of his friends — Durrance, Trench and Castleton — accuse Harry of leaving the military out of cowardice, and he receives a white feather, symbolizing his disgrace, from each of them. After a sense of shame kills his father, Harry travels to Africa, determined to redeem himself. Learning that one of his friends, Capt. Trench, has been captured and is being held prisoner in a fortress, Harry

The Four Feathers

attempts to free him, but is imprisoned himself. They are bought by a slave trader, but Harry kills the trader. After he and Trench endure and survive various perils during their escape (including savage tribesmen, a brush fire and a stampede of hippopotami), they are rescued by British soldiers in the Sudan.

After Harry returns the feathers to Durrance and Trench, the British fort is attacked by tribesmen. Harry redeems himself by killing their chief as Castleton leads a relief column against the tribe. The four later return to England, where they are decorated for their bravery in battle and Harry is reunited with Ethne.

Comments: A part-silent/part-talkie, *The Four Feathers* is largely silent in terms of dialogue, but benefits greatly from a Movietone track containing a synchronized orchestral score and sound effects. A traditional silent version of the film was also prepared by Paramount for exhibition in theaters not yet converted to sound. There have been many subsequent film and television adaptations of A. E. W. Mason's stirring novel of cowardice and redemption in war, the most famous being the 1939 British version, filmed in Technicolor. But this Paramount version of 1929 is excellent in its own right, despite the "handicap" of its part-silent, part-sound status. This is probably the main reason why the film is no longer considered commercially viable. Along with most of the other Paramount features from 1928 to 1948 (this block contains all of the Paramount movies W. C. Fields, The Marx Brothers, Mae West, Bob Hope and director Billy Wilder made in those years), *The Four Feathers* is owned by Universal Pictures; after early television distribution, it has languished in their vaults. In a 1988 interview with co-author Kinnard, Wray commented: "When I first went to Paramount, it was during the transitional period from silent to sound, and the burden of that was pretty heavy on the studio, I think, and they hardly knew how to deal with it. That reflected on a great many of us who were there, and I found circumstances very uncomfortable." *The Four Feathers* was Wray's first collaboration with the filmmaking team of Merian C. Cooper and Ernest B. Schoedsack, later to cast her in *The Most Dangerous Game* and *King Kong*.

Thunderbolt

Paramount, 1929; *Released:* June 22, 1929; *Associate Producer:* B. P. Fineman; *Director:* Josef von Sternberg; *Screenplay:* Jules Furthman, Story by Charles Furthman, Jules Furthman; *Titles:* Herman J. Mankiewicz, Joseph L. Mankiewicz, Josef von Sternberg; *Photography:* Henry Gerrard; *Sets:* Hans Dreier; *Film Editor:* Helen Lewis; *Music:* Karl Hajos, Song "Thinkin' About My Baby" by Sam Coslow; *Recording Engineer:* M. M. Paggi (84 minutes)

Cast: George Bancroft ("Thunderbolt" Jim Lang), Fay Wray ("Ritzi"), Richard Arlen (Bob Morgan), Tully Marshall (Warden), Eugenie Besserer (Mrs. Morgan), James Spottswood ("Snapper" O'Shea), Fred Kohler ("Bad" Al Frieberg), Robert Elliott (Prison Chaplain), E. H. Calvert (District Attorney McKay),

Part II. Sound Films

***Thunderbolt*:** With George Bancroft

George Irving (Mr. Corwin), Mike Donlin (Kentucky Sampson), S. S. Stewart (Black Convict), William L. Thorne (Police Inspector), Elmer Ballard

Synopsis: Gangster "Thunderbolt" Jim Lang is told by his gun moll Ritzi (FW) that she is leaving him and going straight. Lang's hoods discover that Ritzi is now living with the mother of Bob Morgan, the bank clerk she loves. Afraid that Lang may try to kill Bob, Ritzi informs on Lang and helps the police to capture him. Lang is tried and sentenced to death for his crimes, but from prison he frames Bob Morgan for a robbery. Wrongly convicted, Bob is confined to a cell near Lang's. Lang tries to reach Bob and kill him before he himself is executed, but eventually realizes that he was wrong. Lang admits that he framed Bob and repents before going to his own death.

Comments: This underworld crime melodrama was directed by Josef von Sternberg, who would soon travel to Berlin and make *The Blue Angel* with Marlene Dietrich. Josef von Sternberg's direction in *Thunderbolt* is the film's main point of interest today. *Variety*, reviewing the film on June 26, found the movie "another gangster picture that looks like most of the others until about the halfway mark, when the action is transplanted to the death cell of a penitentiary. Richard Arlen ... and Fay Wray ... both impress." *Thunderbolt* was riding the crest of a developing wave of gangster and crime dramas; Warner Bros. would release *Little Caesar* the following year, and the trend would continue until the mid–30s. A silent version of *Thunderbolt* was also distributed. As for Fay Wray, she was not entirely happy with her tenure at Paramount. She told co-author Kinnard in 1988: "I felt I was very restricted by very circumscribed stories, and put into things that didn't suit me and I didn't suit. It went both ways. I think *Legion of the Condemned* had certain elements that were good for me. That was my first film at Paramount. There were some good things about *Street of Sin*, but they were cut out. And then I did *Pointed Heels*. I didn't belong in that. I don't think I belonged as a gangster's moll in *Thunderbolt*. They were pretty clichéd stories, and it was kind of impersonal."

Pointed Heels

Paramount, 1929; *Released:* December 21, 1929; *Director:* A. Edward Sutherland, Screenplay, Adaptation and Dialogue: Florence Ryerson, John V. A. Weaver, From the story "Pointed Heels" by Charles William Brackett, published in *College Humor*; *Dialogue Director:* Perry Ivins; *Photography:* Rex Wimpy (Technicolor inserts); *Film Editor:* Jane Loring, Song "I Have to Have You" by Richard A. Whiting, Leo Robin, Song "Ain't-Cha?" by Mack Gordon, Max Rich, Music: W. Franke Harling; *Sound:* Harry M. Lindgren (61 minutes)

Cast: William Powell (Robert Courtland), Fay Wray (Lora Nixon), Helen Kane (Dot Nixon), Richard "Skeets" Gallagher (Dash Nixon), Phillips Holmes (Donald Ogden), Adrienne Dore (Kay Wilcox), Eugene Pallette (Joe Clark)

Synopsis: Chorus girl Lora Nixon (FW) walks out on a musical show produced by Robert Courtland, who has a romantic interest in her, when she marries struggling composer Donald Ogden. Donald's wealthy family cuts him off financially after he marries Lora, and out of necessity Lora returns to the chorus as Donald continues to pursue success as a songwriter. Courtland attempts to break up their marriage. After Lora visits Courtland in his apartment, she decides to leave Donald. They are finally reunited, though, after a song Donald has written for one of Courtland's shows is a hit.

Comments: In this backstage theater drama, William Powell (still five years away from *The Thin Man*) commands most of the dramatics and the footage, interrupted by musical numbers and technicolor inserts. *Variety* commented

"You can't Don – Oh! – you can't..."

Pointed Heels: With Phillips Holmes

in their January 1, 1930 review: "Miss Wray and Phillips Holmes as the young married couple make no more than an ordinary impression in their scattered appearances.... Technicolor sequence, production number in the show, runs about three minutes and is hazily unimportant except for possible exploitation." A silent version of *Pointed Heels* was also distributed.

Behind the Make-Up

Paramount, 1930; *Released:* January 11, 1930; *Director:* Robert Milton; *Screenplay, Adaptation and Dialogue:* George Manker Watters, Howard Estabrook, From the

Behind the Make-Up portrait

story "The Feeder" by Mildred Cram, published in *Redbook*; *Photography:* Charles Lang; *Film Editor:* Doris Drought, Songs "My Pals," "Say It With Your Feet," "I'll Remember, You'll Forget" by Leo Robin, Sam Coslow, Newell Chase; *Recording Engineer:* Harry D. Mills (70 minutes)

Cast: Hal Skelly (Hap Brown), William Powell (Gardoni), Fay Wray (Marie), Kay Francis (Kitty Parker), E. H. Calvert (Dawson), Paul Lukas (Boris), Agostino Borgato (Chef), Jacques Vanaire (Valet), Jean De Briac (Sculptor) Torben Meyer (Waiter), Bob Perry (Bartender)

Synopsis: Actor Hap Brown is in love with Marie (FW), a waitress in the French Quarter of New Orleans. Brown meets Gardoni, a fellow actor down on his luck; they form a partnership and establish an act, but soon part company when Gardoni insists on more control. When Hap reteams with Gardoni later on, Marie falls for Gardoni and they are married. Hap's career wanes, and Gardoni is unfaithful to Marie, cheating on her with Kitty Parker. Although the rejected Hap knows of Gardoni's infidelity, he decides not to tell Marie. Gardoni dies after Kitty leaves him, and Hap becomes a successful comedian under Marie's influence after they get back together.

Comments: This Paramount film was Wray's third appearance in a movie with William Powell. She told co-author Kinnard in 1988 that Powell was one of her favorite co-stars.

Paramount on Parade

Paramount, 1930; *Released:* April 19, 1930; *Supervisor:* Elsie Janis; *Directors:* Dorothy Arzner, Otto Brower, Edmund Goulding, Victor Heerman, Edwin H. Knopf, Rowland V. Lee, Ernst Lubitsch, Lothar Mendes, Victor Schertzinger, Edward Sutherland, Frank Tuttle, Photography (Technicolor inserts): Harry Fischbeck, Victor Milner; *Set Designer:* John Wenger, Songs "Paramount on Parade Theme Song," "Any Time's the Time to Fall in Love," "What Did Cleopatra Say?," "I'm True to the Navy Now" by Elsie Janis, Jack King, Song "We're the Masters of Ceremony" by Ballard MacDonald, Dave Dreyer, Song "Torma a Sorrento" by Leo Robin, Ernesto DeCurtis, Songs "I'm in Training for You," "Dancing to Save Your Sole," "Let Us Drink to the Girl of My Dreams" by L. Wolfe Gilbert, Abel Baer, Song "My Marine" by Richard A. Whiting, Raymond B. Eagan, Song "All I Want Is Just One Girl" by Richard A. Whiting, Leo Robin, Song "I'm Isadore, the Toreador" by David Franklin, Song "Sweepin' the Clouds Away" by Sam Coslow; *Dance and Ensemble Director:* David Bennett (102 minutes)

Part II. Sound Films

Paramount on Parade portrait

Cast (listed alphabetically, appearing as themselves): Iris Adrian, Richard Arlen, Jean Arthur, Mischa Auer, William Austin, George Bancroft, Clara Bow, Evelyn Brent, Mary Brian, Clive Brook, Virginia Bruce, Nancy Carroll, Ruth Chatterton, Maurice Chevalier, Gary Cooper, Cecil Cunningham, Leon Errol, Stuart Erwin, Henry Fink, Kay Francis, Skeets Gallagher, Edmund Goulding,

Harry Green, Mitzi Green, Robert Grieg, James Hall, Phillips Holmes, Helen Kane, Dennis King, Abe Lyman and His Band, Fredric March, Nino Martini, Mitzi Mayfair, Marion Morgan Dancers, David Newell, Jack Oakie, Warner Oland, Zelma O'Neal, Eugene Pallette, Joan Peters, Jack Pennick, William Powell, Charles "Buddy" Rogers, Lillian Roth, Rolfe Sedan, Stanley Smith, Fay Wray

Synopsis: An all-star musical revue, designed to showcase Paramount's contract talent for the new medium of talking pictures.

Comments: Wray is glimpsed only briefly in the available television prints, appearing in a black-and-white introduction to a missing Technicolor sequence in which she performed with Richard Arlen, Jean Arthur, Mary Brian, Gary Cooper and James Hall.

The Texan

Paramount, 1930; *Released:* May 10, 1930; *Director:* John Cromwell; *Screenplay:* Daniel Nathan Rubin; *Adaptation:* Oliver H. P. Garrett, From the story "The Double-Eyed Deceiver" by O. Henry, published in *Everybody's Magazine* in December 1905; *Photography:* Victor Milner, Film Editor: Verna Willis, Songs "Chico" and "To Hold You" by L. Wolfe Gilbert, Abel Baer; *Recording Engineer:* Harry M. Lindgren (79 minutes)

Cast: Gary Cooper ("Quico," The Llano Kid), Fay Wray (Consuelo), Emma Dunn (Senora Ibarra), Oscar Apfel (Thacker), James Marcus (Sheriff John Brown), Donald Reed (Nick Ibarra), Soledad Jimenez (Duenna), Veda Buckland (Mary, Nurse), Cesar Vanoni (Pasquale), Edwin J. Brady (Henry), Enrique Acosta (Sixto), Romulado Tirado (Cabman)

Synopsis: The Llano Kid, a young bandit wanted by the law, kills a card cheat in self-defense while they are involved in a poker game with Sheriff John Brown. The Kid escapes, pursued by Sheriff Brown. Aboard a train The Kid meets Thacker, a crook who convinces him to masquerade as the son of Senora Ibarra, a rich South American widow whose real son disappeared as a boy.

The Kid successfully pretends to be her long-lost son Enrique, planning to help Thacker steal the widow's gold. Then he falls in love with Consuelo, Enrique Ibarra's niece, and learns that the real Enrique Ibarra was the man he killed in the poker game. He refuses to continue with Thacker's scheme.

Sheriff Brown tracks down the Llano Kid. The Kid is wounded and Thacker is killed in a shootout when Thacker and his gang try to steal Senora Ibarra's gold.

***The Border Legion*:** Candid, on location

Learning of The Kid's love for Consuelo, Sheriff Brown agrees to report Thacker's death as that of The Llano Kid, allowing The Kid to continue his romance with Consuelo.

Comments: On May 21, 1930, *Variety* praised this Paramount production: "Few westerns are as well-made and rate as high in every particular, including entertainment and production value, as *The Texan*."

The Border Legion

Paramount, 1930; *Released:* June 28, 1930; *Directors:* Otto Brower, Edwin H. Knopf; *Screenplay:* Percy Heath, Edward E. Paramore, Jr., Based on the novel

The Border Legion by Zane Grey; *Photography:* Mack Stengler; *Film Editor:* Doris Drought; *Recording Engineer:* Earl Hayman (68 minutes)

Cast: Richard Arlen (Jim Cleve), Jack Holt (Jack Kells), Fay Wray (Joan Randall), Eugene Pallette ("Bunco" Davis), Stanley Fields (Hack Gulden), E. H. Calvert (Judge Savin), Ethan Allen (George Randall), Sid Saylor (Shrimp), Hank Bell (Kells Gang Member), Jim Corey (Kells Gang Member)

Synopsis: Jim Cleve, wrongly accused of murdering a local miner, is about to be hung in the town of Alder Creek, Idaho, when he is rescued by Jack Kells, leader of a notorious outlaw gang known as The Border Legion. Grateful, Jim falls in with the Legion. When fellow gang member Hank Gulden kidnaps Joan Randle (FW), Jim is told to guard her. Jim rebels when Jack Kells develops an interest in Joan, and leaves to oppose the gang. When Hank Gulden tries to kill Jim and Joan, Jack Kells shoots Gulden and is fatally wounded himself, allowing Jim and Joan to escape.

Comments: The Border Legion was a remake of a 1924 Paramount film of the same title, starring Antonio Moreno and Helene Chadwick.

The Sea God

Paramount, 1930; *Released:* September 13, 1930; *Director-Screenplay-Dialogue:* George Abbott, Based on the story "The Lost God" by John Russell; *Photography:* Archie Stout; *Original Music:* Karl Hajos, Stephen Pasternacki, Ralph Rainger; *Sound:* Earl Hayman (75 minutes)

Cast: Richard Arlen (Phillip "Pink" Barker), Fay Wray (Daisy), Eugene Pallette ("Square Deal" McCarthy), Robert Gleckler (Big Schultz), Ivan Simpson (Pearly Nick), Maurice Black (Rudy), Robert Perry (Abe), Fred Wallace (Bill), Willie Fung (Sin Lee), Sol K. Gregory (Duke), Mary De Bow (Mary), James Spencer (Sanaka Joe)

Synopsis: Phillip Barker, a South Seas trader, and Big Schultz, his rival, are both romantically involved with Daisy (FW), who agrees to marry the dishonest Schultz only because he offers the desperate girl a job in his general store. Learning about a sunken treasure of pearls from a man he rescues at sea, Barker sets sail in pursuit of the treasure. Big Schultz hears about the treasure and follows Barker in another ship. Daisy, who really loves Barker, has stowed away on his ship. While Barker is in a deep-sea diving suit searching for the treasure underwater, cannibals attack his ship, killing most of the crew and kidnapping Daisy and McCarthy, the first mate. Barker, still underwater and unable to resurface

The Sea God: With Richard Arlen

***The Sea God*:** With Richard Arlen

without assistance, walks along the seabed until he appears ashore on the island where Daisy and McCarthy are held captive by the cannibals. Big Schultz and his men arrive on the island, and are killed by the cannibals. Barker is able to escape with Daisy and McCarthy when the cannibals see Barker in his diving suit and mistake him for a god.

Comments: The Sea God was shot on location at Santa Catalina Island and in the Channel Islands, with cinematographer Archie Stout, a low-budget B-Western perennial (he shot many of John Wayne's early movies), contributing some nice effects. Director-scenarist George Abbott (who enjoyed a long theatrical career, and lived to see his hundredth birthday), kept the simplistic plot moving at a brisk pace, using his solid cast to good advantage. When *The Sea God* was produced, recording technology had not advanced sufficiently to allow the economical dubbing of movies for foreign release, so foreign versions of movies, using different actors on the same sets, were quickly made for the export market. The Spanish version of *The Sea God* (*El Dios del Mar*) was directed by Francisco Moreno and Edward D. Venturini, photographed by David Abel, and starred Manuel Arbo, Paco Moreno and Rosita Moreno. *Variety*, reviewing *The Sea God* on September 10, commented, "Readers of adventure mags and the red-blooded youth of the land will like [it] ... theme is an old one grafted onto several other old ones ... but it doesn't pretend to be anything but hoke."

Captain Thunder

Warner Bros., 1930; *Released:* December 27, 1930; *Director:* Alan Crosland; *Screenplay:* Gordon Rigby, Based on the story "The Gay Caballero" by Pierre Couderc and Hal Devitt, Dialogue: William K. Wells; *Photography:* James Van Trees; *Film Editor:* Arthur Hilton; *Music:* Erno Rapee; *Music Conductor:* Louis Silvers; *Sound Engineer:* George R. Groves (66 minutes)

Cast: Fay Wray (Ynez Dominguez), Victor Varconi (Captain Thunder), Charles Judels (Commandante Ruiz), Robert Elliott (Pete Morgan), Don Alvarado (Juan Sebastian), Natalie Moorhead (Bonita Salazar), Bert Roach (Pablo), Frank Campeau (Hank Riley), Robert Emmett Keane (Don Miguel Salazar), John Sainpolis (Pedro Dominguez), Soledad Jimenez (Mrs. Ruiz)

Synopsis: The people of El Paramo demand that Commandant Ruiz pursue and capture El Capitan Tronido ("Captain Thunder"), a dashing Mexican bandit. Young lovers Ynez Dominguez (FW) and Juan Sebastion intend to marry, but Ynez's father wants her to marry Pete Morgan, a wealthy American rancher. Aware of this, Juan tells Ynez that he plans to track down Captain Thunder so that he can collect the reward and they can elope. Juan captures the wily bandit and prepares to marry Ynez. Captain Thunder escapes and Morgan, whom Cap-

Part II. Sound Films

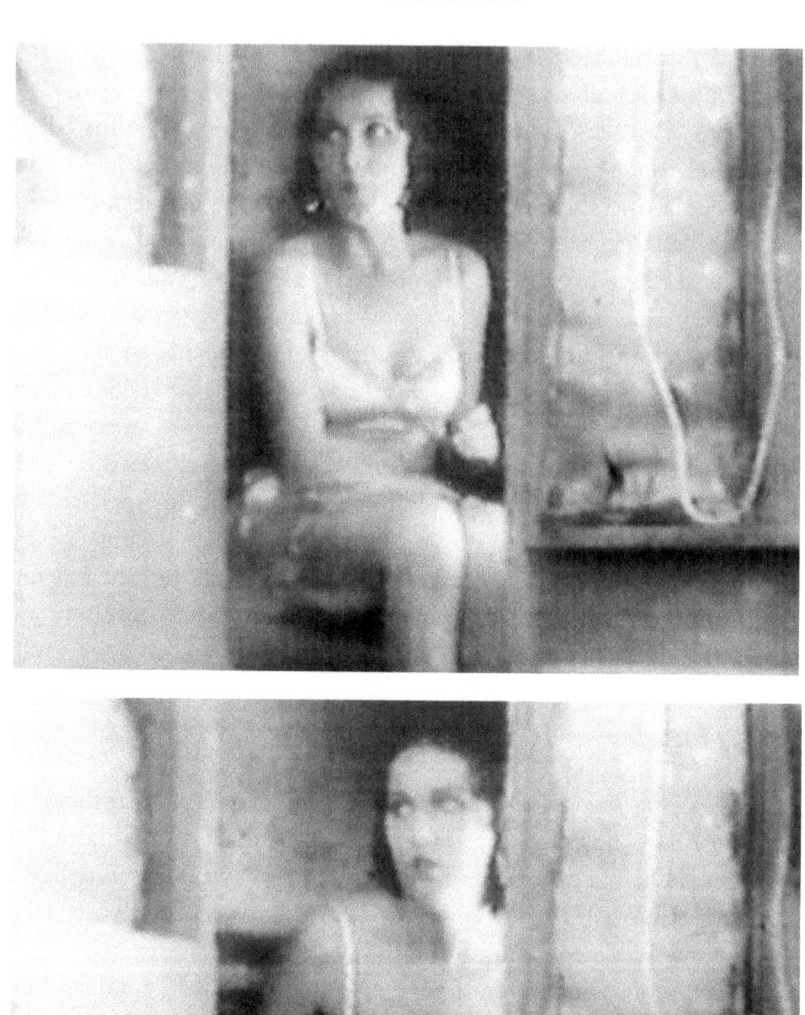

Captain Thunder frame enlargements

tain Thunder has met and is indebted to, forces the bandito to prevent Ynez's wedding. But after Morgan marries Ynez, Captain Thunder fatally shoots the rancher, allowing Ynez and Juan to continue their romance.

Comments: This south-of-the-border drama found Wray improbably cast as a Mexican senorita who becomes romantically involved with the notorious bandit El Capitan Tronido (Captain Thunder). Some critics felt that Wray's performance here was not very good, and found her ethnic characterization unconvincing. This pre–Code film contains a slightly risqué scene of Wray in her underwear, a sequence that would have been suppressed only a few years later, once Hollywood censorship was tightened. The working title for this film was *The Gay Caballero*.

The Conquering Horde

Paramount, 1931; *Released:* March 7, 1931; *Director:* Edward Sloman; *Screenplay:* Grover Jones, William Slavens McNutt, Based on the novel *North of 36* by Emerson Hough; *Photography:* Archie Stout; *Music:* Sigmund Krumgold, John Leipold, Ralph Rainger; *Film Editor:* Otho Lovering; *Sound Engineer:* Harold Lewis (76 minutes)

Cast: Richard Arlen (Dan McMasters), Fay Wray (Taisie Lockhart), Claude Gillingwater (Jim Nabours), Ian McLaren (Marvin Fletcher), George Mendoza (Cinco Centavos), James Durkin (Mr. Amos Corley), Arthur Stone ("Lumpy" Lorrigan), Frank Rice ("Spud" Grogan), Charles Stevens (John), Edwin J. Brady (Splint Grogan), Robert Kortman (Digger Hale), Harry Cording (Butch Daggett), Chief Standing Bear (Blue Cloud), John Elliott (Capt. Wilkins), Katherine Clare Ward (Mrs. Corley)

The Conquering Horde portrait

"Why should you understand – you're a woman in a man's country"

The Conquering Horde

Part II. Sound Films

Synopsis: Ranchers in post–Civil War Texas are in financial difficulty when the Union Pacific Railroad bypasses their land. Preying on the desperate ranchers, State Treasurer Marvin Fletcher begins buying their land for three cents an acre; Taisie Lockhart (FW), owner of the Laguna del Sol Ranch, refuses to sell. Union veteran Dan McMasters returns from the war, intending to resume his romance with Taisie, but she rejects him because he fought against the South. Dan does not tell her that he has another reason for returning home: At the request of the President, he is secretly investigating Fletcher's crooked business dealings.

Jim Nabours, one of Taisie's ranch hands, has an angry confrontation with Fletcher that leads to a gunfight, but Dan stops this by shooting Nabours' gun from his hand. Although he has provoked Nabours' enmity, Dan uses the incident as a pretext to meet Fletcher and gain his confidence. Dan hatches a scheme to save the poverty-stricken ranchers when he asks Taisie to run her cattle herd to Abilene, where she can sell for top dollar, believing the other ranchers will then follow her example and do the same. Dan, hired by Taisie as a guide, rides with the herd to Abilene, but the crooked Fletcher and his gang follow them, provoking warfare between the cattlemen and nearby Indian tribes. One of Taisie's ranch hands rides to summon the Cavalry, and the Indian uprising is prevented. Fletcher, who provoked the Indian attack, is turned over to the tribe to face Native American justice. Taisie is then able to drive the herd to Abilene, her romance with Dan McMasters rekindled.

Comments: This western drama of post–Civil War hardships brought about by the expanding railroad was filmed under the title *Stampede*. *The Conquering Horde* was a remake of a 1924 Paramount silent, *North of 36*, directed by Irvin Willat and starring Jack Holt.

Not Exactly Gentlemen

Fox, 1931; *Released:* March 8, 1931; *Producer:* William Fox; *Associate Producer:* Edmund Grainger; *Director:* Benjamin Stoloff; *Screenplay:* William Conselman, Dudley Nichols, Hayden Talbot, Based on the novel *Over the Border* by Herman Whitaker; *Continuity:* Emmett Flynn; *Photography:* Daniel Clark; *Set Design:* William Darling; *Film Editor:* Milton Carruth; *Costumes:* Sophie Wachner, Earl Mosner; *Music:* Peter Brunelli, Arthur Kay, Jean Talbot, Jack Virgil; *Sound Engineer:* A. L. Kirbach; *Assistant Directors:* Ewing Scott, Earl Rettig; *Riding Doubles and Stunt Riders:* Kermit Maynard, Cliff Lyons, Jack Duane (Double for Robert

Not Exactly Gentlemen: With Victor McLaglen

Warwick), Frank Ellis (Double for Edward Gribbon), Audrey Scott (Double for Fay Wray) (61 minutes)

Cast: Victor McLaglen (Bull Stanley), Fay Wray (Lee Carleton), Lew Cody (Ace Beaudry), Robert Warwick (Layne Hunter), Edward Gribbon (Bronco Dawson), David Worth (Bruce Randall), Joyce Compton (Ace's Girl), Louise Huntington (Bronco's girl), Franklyn Farnum (Nelson), Carol Wines (Bull's Girl), James Farley (Marshall Dunn), Shorty Wood, George Williams, Jack Martin, Pete Morrison, W. H. Moseley, Gordon Jones, Charles Johnson, Leslie Cooper, Rex Cole, Roscoe Baden, C. C. O'Neal, Fox O'Callahan, Bob Newsom, George Newsom, Fat Reynolds, Archie Ricks, Clint Sharp, Jack Sanders, Bob Slaughter, Pete Genant, Charles Springer, Lenthal McCoy, Otto Meyer, B. M. Moseley, Lee Peterson, Allen Lee, R. E. Lee, Tex Palmer, Earl Dobbins, Bob Erickson, John Erlich, Press Firth, Bob Geerhart, Hank Groves, Slim Hightower, George Hunter (Teamsters), Budd Timmons, Henry Morris (Horsemen), Harry Mount (Bugler), Joe Ray, Cliff Lyons, Jack Duane, Victor De Linsky, Frank Ellis (Deputies), Joe Rickson, Bill Patton, Vester Pegg (Henchmen), Roy Stewart, Luke Cosgrave, Allen Lee

Synopsis: Thieves Ace Beaudry, Bronco Dawson and Bull Stanley travel west and attempt to steal a team of thoroughbred horses leading a wagon near the town of Custer, where crowds are gathering to embark on a land rush. Layne Hunter, a crooked saloon owner from Custer, attacks the wagon with his gang, but they are driven off by the three bandits. Before they can steal the horses, though, Ace and his friends discover Lee Carleton (FW). Lee, whose father died in the fight, innocently believes that the three men have rescued her and tells them that she had been traveling with her father to file a claim on a gold mine. Seeing a chance to acquire her mine, the trio accompanies Lee to Custer and secretly agree that one of them must marry her. Lee is not interested in any of the three men romantically, though. Nelson, Layne Hunter's associate, learns of the gold mine and they kidnap Lee, stealing her map to the mine.

Bull Stanley and Bruce Randall, Lee's newly arrived Eastern fiancé, rescue Lee. Having committed the map to memory, she leads them to the mine. A violent gunfight erupts, with Bull, Bronco, Ace and Bruce defeating Hunter and his gang. Grateful, Lee offers to share her mine claim with the three men, but seeing that the Marshall is approaching, they simply wave goodbye to Lee and Bruce, riding off empty-handed and one step ahead of the law.

Comments: Not Exactly Gentlemen was filmed under the working titles *Land Rush, Three Rough Diamonds* and *Three Bad Men.* The film was initially released in New York as *Three Rogues* before the title was finally changed to *Not Exactly Gentlemen* for general release. It was a remake of Fox's 1926 film *Three Bad Men,* directed by John Ford and starring George O'Brien and Olive Borden.

Dirigible

Columbia, 1931; *Released:* April 4, 1931; *Producer:* Harry Cohn; *Director:* Frank Capra; *Screenplay:* Frank Wilber Wead, USN; *Adaptation and Dialogue:* Jo Swerling; *Continuity:* Dorothy Howell; *Photography:* Joseph Walker, with Frank Zucker, Andre Barlatier, Charles Levine, Rube Boyce, George Meehan, Victor Scheurich, Al Wertzel; *Aerial Photography:* Elmer Dyer; *Sets:* Edward C. Jewell, Edward Shulter; *Film Editors:* Maurice Wright, Harry Decker; *Music Arrangements:* Constantin Bakaleinikoff, David Broekman; *Sound Engineer:* John Livadar; *Sound Assistants:* Edward Bernds, Dan Milner, Edward Wetzel, Edward C. Hahn; *Chief Electrician:* Denver Harmon; *Assistant Grip:* George Hager; *Special Effects:* Ned Mann, W. J. Butler; *Assistant Director:* Sam Nelson; *General Studio Manager:* Samuel J. Briskin; *Unit Manager:* Joe Cooke (100 minutes)

Cast: Jack Holt (Commander Jack Bradon), Ralph Graves (Lt. Frisky Pierce), Fay Wray (Helen Pierce), Hobart Bosworth (Louis Rondelle), Roscoe Karns (Sock MacGuire), Harold Goodwin (Hansen), Clarence Muse (Clarence, the Waiter), Emmet Corrigan (Rear Admiral John S. Martin), Alan Roscoe (Commander of U.S.S. *Lexington*), Selmer Jackson (Lt. Rowland)

Synopsis: Jack Bradon, commander of the U.S. Navy's dirigible fleet, is determined to use his airships to aid explorer Louis Rondelle on his expedition to the South Pole. Bradon stages a demonstration of his dirigibles' capabilities to impress Rondelle, who agrees to use the airships. Bradon is secretly in love with Helen Pierce (FW), the neglected wife of one of his pilots, Lt. Frisky Pierce. When Helen learns of the South Pole expedition, she is so fearful for her husband's safety that she begs Bradon to tell Frisky that he cannot go, which Bradon does out of respect for Helen. When Bradon's dirigible is disabled in a storm, Frisky flies to his rescue in a plane, and both of them return to Washington, D. C. Frisky resigns from the Navy so that he can join Rondelle's South Pole expedition.

Resigned to this, Helen gives Frisky a letter that she tells him to open at the South Pole; in it she has written that she has had enough of his neglect, and that she intends to divorce him and marry Jack Bradon. Frisky, oblivious to Helen's feelings, flies to the South Pole, where his plane crashes. Bradon realizes from Helen's emotional reaction to the news that she is still in love with Frisky. Frisky, Rondelle and the others, stranded at the South Pole, slowly make their way across the frozen wasteland. One by one they succumb to the bitter cold, but Frisky is eventually rescued when Bradon flies to the South Pole in his dirigible. Frisky, snow-blind from his ordeal, remembers Helen's letter and asks Jack to read it for him. Jack makes up a fictitious love letter from Helen, disposing of the real letter. They return to New York, where Frisky is reunited with Helen.

Comments: Dirigible, budgeted at $1,000,000, was a prestige film and an important production for Harry Cohn's fledgling Columbia Pictures, as well as for up-and- coming director Frank Capra. Essentially a man's action picture in the *Hell's Angels* mold, it deals with the dirigible expedition and its toll (psychological as well as physical) on those involved. *Dirigible* was the first screenwriting effort of Commander Frank Wilber Wead. The former World War I Navy pilot, who authored many subsequent pictures in the same vein, was profiled (as played by John Wayne) in the 1957 biopic *The Wings of Eagles,* directed by John Ford for MGM. *Variety* said of *Dirigible* on April 8: "Of the actors Fay Wray looks the best. Miss Wray is earnestly sincere as the wife of the glory-seeking aviator...." Despite the review's kindness, Wray's part was minimal and rather thankless as her character listened to radio reports in a stuffy apartment, awaiting news of her husband (Graves). *Dirigible* was the first of many Columbia films in which Wray would appear. More than one source has erroneously stated that Wray posed for the familiar Columbia lady-with-a-torch studio logo, but when co-author Kinnard asked her about this in 1988, she stated emphatically that it was untrue.

The Finger Points

First National, 1931; *Released:* April 11, 1931; *Producer-Director:* John Francis Dillon; *Screenplay:* John Monk Saunders, W. R. Burnett; *Adaptation:* Robert Lord; *Dialogue:* John Monk Saunders; *Photography:* Ernest Haller; *Art Director:* Jack Okey; *Film Editor:* LeRoy Stone; *Sound:* Dolph Thomas; *Costumes:* Earl Luick; *Vitaphone Orchestra Conductor:* David Mendoza; *Music:* Chopin's *Funeral March* (88 minutes)

Cast: Richard Barthelmess (Breckinridge Lee), Fay Wray (Marcia Collins), Regis Toomey (Charles "Breezy" Russell), Robert Elliott (Frank Carter), Clark Gable (Louis Blanco), Oscar Apfel (Managing Editor Wheeler), Robert Gleckler (Larry Hays), Mickey Bennett (Office Boy), Noel Madison (Larry Hayes [scenes deleted]), Lew Harvey (Henchman), Herman Krumpfel (Breck's Tailor), Frank Marlowe (Guard), J. Carrol Naish (Phone Voice), Bob Perry (Guard)

Synopsis: Newspaper reporter Breckinridge Lee is assaulted by mobsters after he tries to write a story about a gambling house. Lee plans to marry fellow reporter Marcia Collins (FW), but they have a falling out when he agrees to accept a bribe from mobster Louis Blanco, and she objects to the source of his newfound wealth. When Marcia decides to marry another reporter, Charles "Breezy" Russell, Lee tells her that he will reform and break off his mob ties if she will take him back. Marcia agrees. Lee is murdered after writing a story about a new mob-affiliated gambling house. He is eulogized as a hero at his funeral, and Marcia, aware of his mob ties, keeps the truth to herself out of love and respect.

Comments: This hard-hitting newspaper story was based on a contemporary real-life incident: the murder of *Chicago Tribune* reporter Jake Lingle by Al Capone's mob, just as Lingle was about to discuss the mobster's activities with federal agents. The screenplay was co-written by Wray's husband John Monk Saunders, and far down in the cast list was newcomer Clark Gable. Wray had no scenes with Gable.

The Lawyer's Secret

Paramount, 1931; *Released:* June 6, 1931; *Directors:* Louis Gasnier, Max Marcin; *Screenplay:* Lloyd Corrigan, Max Marcin, James Hilary Finn; *Photography:* Arthur Todd; *Music:* Jay Gorney, Karl Hajos, John Leipold; *Lyrics:* E. Y. Harburg; *Sound Engineer:* J. A. Goodrich (65 minutes)

Cast: Clive Brook (Drake Norris), Charles Rogers (Laurie Roberts), Richard Arlen (Joe Hart), Fay Wray (Kay Roberts), Jean Arthur (Beatrice Stevens), Francis McDonald ("The Weasel"), Harold Goodwin ("Madame X"), Syd Saylor ("Red"), Laurence La Marr (Tom), Robert Perry (Baldy), Wilbur Mack (District Attorney), Sheila Bromley, G. Pat Collins, Claire Dodd, Edward LeSaint

Synopsis: Sailor Joe Hart loses all of his money in a gambling dive and sells his gun to a man named Laurie Roberts in order to raise cash. When Hart loses the money Roberts paid him for the gun, he leaves and steals a car so that he can get back to his ship. "The Weasel," a gambler, tells Laurie that Baldy, the owner of the gambling joint, is dishonest. Laurie, who also lost money there, returns with The Weasel to rob the safe. When Baldy confronts them, The Weasel shoots him with Hart's gun.

Laurie's sister Kay (FW) asks her fiancé, attorney Drake Norris, to speak with Laurie about his shady friends. Laurie confidentially admits his knowledge of Baldy's murder to Norris, who tells him that he could be prosecuted as an accomplice.

Hart is tried, found guilty and sentenced to hang. His girlfriend Beatrice implores Norris to appeal the verdict. Norris declines and, without revealing to Kay her brother's role in the murder, admits to her that he has been given confidential information by an unnamed client regarding the killing. Laurie, assuming that Norris has told Kay everything, reveals the truth, and Kay begs Norris to take Laurie's case. Without identifying Laurie, Norris visits the governor, unsuccessfully seeking a pardon for Hart. The Weasel is eventually identified as the real murderer, and Laurie admits that he had bought the murder weapon from Hart. Hart is freed, The Weasel is sentenced to death and Laurie receives a relatively light prison sentence.

Comments: This sparse crime drama, running just over an hour, was Wray's tenth film under her Paramount contract.

The Unholy Garden

Goldwyn–United Artists, 1931; *Released:* October 10, 1931; *Producer:* Samuel Goldwyn, *Director:* George Fitzmaurice, *Screenplay:* Ben Hecht, Charles MacArthur,

The Unholy Garden: With Ronald Colman

Part II. Sound Films

The Unholy Garden

John Lee Mahin; *Photography:* George S. Barnes, Gregg Toland; *Set Design:* Richard Day, Willy Pogany; *Film Editor:* Grant Whytock; *Supervising Editor:* Stuart Heisler; *Sound:* Frank Grenzback; *Music:* Alfred Newman (75 minutes)

Cast: Ronald Colman (Barrington Hunt), Fay Wray (Camille deJonghe), Estelle Taylor (Elise Mowbry), Warren Hymer (Smiley Corbin), Tully Marshall (Baron Louis deJonghe), Lawrence Grant (Dr. Shayne), Ullrich Haupt (Col. Von Axt), Kit Guard (Kid Twist), Henry Armetta (Nick the Goose), Lucille La Verne (Mme. Lucie Villars), Mischa Auer (Prince Nicolai Poliakoff), Henry Kolker (Col. Lautrac), Charles H. Mailes (Alfred), William von Brincken, Morgan Wallace (Capt. Kruger), Arnold Korff (Commandant Louis Lautrac), Nadja (Native Dancer)

Synopsis: Bank robber Barrington Hunt and his accomplice Smiley Corbin leave Paris after their latest criminal endeavor. They wind up in the city of Orage in Algeria, then journey through the desert to the Palais Royale, a notorious den of thieves where criminals gather without interference from the law. Hunt and

Part II. Sound Films

Corbin are accepted by the morley crew in residence. When the other hoods at the Palais Royale discover that Baron Louis deJonghe, an elderly, disabled guest, has a large amount of stolen money, they decide to murder him. Hunt decides that it would be be wiser to romance the old man's innocent daughter Camille (FW) in an effort to steal the loot. Hunt gradually falls in love with Camille. When her father is murdered by one of the criminals, Col. Von Axt, they escape.

Leaving the Palais Royale behind them, Hunt tells Camille that he is not good enough for her, and gives her all of her father's money. Promising to return when he feels that he is worthy of her love, he leaves with Smiley Corbin.

Comments: In this prestigious Samuel Goldwyn production, Wray (in blonde hair) looked beautiful and interacted well with star Colman. The film is well-photographed by George S. Barnes, with additional camerawork by Gregg Toland, who would shoot *Citizen Kane* a decade later. The film is somewhat inconsistent visually; after negative audience response at previews, some scenes were reshot by Toland and intercut with Barnes' previous work. Sets were by Willy Pogany, who would design the classic Boris Karloff film *The Mummy* at Universal the following year. In a conversation with co-author Kinnard in 1993, Wray expressed disappointment over this film, mainly due to the script, which she considered substandard and somewhat unrealistic. She had been unaware in 1931, and was surprised to learn, that prestigious scripters Ben Hecht and Charles MacArthur had "farmed out" the writing chores on this film to anonymous hands, after becoming more involved with scripting the Howard Hughes production *Scarface* (1932). Nevertheless, *The Unholy Garden* certainly looks good and plays well, holding up better than many early sound films today.

Stowaway

Universal, 1932; *Released:* April 11, 1932; *Producer:* Carl Laemmle; *Associate Producer:* Samuel Freedman; *Director:* Phil Whitman; *Screenplay:* Norman Springer; *Photography:* Leon Shamroy; *Film Editor:* Milton Carruth; *Sound:* C. Roy Hunter; *Music:* David Broekman (75 minutes)

Cast: Fay Wray (Mary Foster), Leon Waycoff [Ames] (Tommy), Montagu Love (First Mate Groder), Lee Moran (Mackie), Roscoe Karns (Inspector Redding), Knute Erickson (Capt. Grant), Paul Porcasi (Tony), Betty Francisco (Madge), James Gordon, Maurice Black

Synopsis: Dance hall girl Mary Foster (FW) is fired when she objects to the flirtatious behavior of Groder, a drunken sailor. Desperate, Mary wanders through

the streets, trailed by a policeman who is about to charge her with prostitution when she loses him and hides aboard a freighter. The ship sets sail with Mary aboard, and she discovers that Groder is first mate. Mary is discovered by Tommy, the second mate, and sleeps with him in his cabin that night. Tommy falls in love with her. In the morning when Groder discovers that she is aboard, Tommy defends her. They fight and Groder dies when, unknown to Tommy and Mary, he is stabbed by Mackie, a sailor Groder had robbed. Tommy is to be turned over to the police and charged with murder

Top: Stowaway *portrait;* ***bottom and opposite:*** Stowaway *poster*

Part II. Sound Films

Stowaway lobby card

when the ship reaches port, but he is cleared when the ship's steward, an undercover customs inspector who had been investigating Groder's criminal activities, reveals that he witnessed Mackie's knifing of Groder.

Comments: Although low-budget, *Stowaway* is a potentially interesting film, both in terms of plot and pre–Code sexual frankness. Unfortunately, the film (like many other Universals from the silent and early sound periods) is no longer generally available for screening. The shooting title, *Tricked*, was changed to *Stowaway* shortly after release. Wray's leading man, Leon Waycoff, later changed his surname to Ames, and is perhaps best known as the perplexed neighbor of Alan Young on the TV sitcom *Mr. Ed*. Production began on February 1, 1932, only ten weeks before release.

Doctor X

First National–Warner Bros., 1932; *Released:* August 27, 1932; *Executive Producers:* Darryl F. Zanuck, Hal B. Wallis; *Director:* Michael Curtiz; *Screenplay:* Robert

Tasker, Earl Baldwin, with contributions by George Rosener; Based on the play *The Terror* by Howard W. Comstock, Allen C. Miller; *Photography (Technicolor version):* Ray Rennahan; *Technicolor Second Cameraman:* W. Howard Greene; *Technicolor Assistant Cameramen:* Thad Brooks, Floyd Lee; *Second Camera:* Carl Guthrie; *Camera:* Ellsworth Fredericks, Ernest Haller, William N. Williams, W. Robinson; *Photography (black-and-white version):* Richard Towers; *Art Director:* Anton Grot; *Film Editor:* George Amy; *Music (Vitaphone Orchestra):* Leo F. Forbstein; *Makeup:* Max Factor, Perc Westmore, Ray Romero; *Special Photographic Effects:* Fred Jackman; *Sound Recording:* Bob Lee; *Hair Stylist:* Ruth Pursley; *Props:* Limey Plews; *Still Photography:* Scotty Welbourne, Grip: Owen Crompton; *Assistant Directors:* Al Alborn, Marshall Hageman; *Technical Advisor:* Dr. C. E. Warriner (80 minutes)

***Doctor X*: With Lionel Atwill**

Cast: Lionel Atwill (Dr. Xavier), Fay Wray (Joan Xavier), Lee Tracy (Lee Taylor), Preston Foster (Dr. Wells), John Wray (Dr. Haines), Harry Beresford (Dr. Duke), Arthur Edmund Carewe (Dr. Rowitz), Leila Bennett (Mamie), Robert Warwick (Stevens), George Rosener (Otto), Willard Robertson (O'Holloran), Thomas Jackson (Editor), Harry Holman (Policeman), Mae Busch (Bordello Madame), Tom Dugan (Sheriff)

Synopsis: New York reporter Lee Taylor investigates a series of grisly cannibalistic murders that take place under the full moon. His investigation leads him to the Blackstone Shoals Medical Academy, supervised by Dr. Xavier, where several eccentric doctors in residence, as well as Xavier himself, fall under suspicion. Matters are complicated when Taylor is attracted to Xavier's daughter Joan (FW). Joan asks Taylor to refrain from publicizing the investigation for the sake of her father's reputation until the murderer is caught, and he agrees.

***Doctor X*:** With Preston Foster (*left*) and Lee Tracy

The police allow Xavier an opportunity to avoid unwanted publicity and capture the murderer on his own. In an effort to do this, Xavier restages one of the crimes, with each of the suspected doctors connected to a complex lie detector mechanism recording each man's heartbeat and pulse rate.

Top: Doctor X: With Lee Tracy; *bottom: Doctor X:* With John Wray.

Part II. Sound Films

***Doctor X*:** With George Rosener

The true murderer is eventually revealed to be Dr. Wells, who has disguised his appearance and even restored his amputated hand with a synthetic flesh compound he has formulated in the laboratory. When Wells reveals his identity and threatens to kill Joan, Taylor intervenes. In the tense struggle that follows, Taylor hurls a kerosene lamp at Wells and the killer bursts into flames, falling through a window and plunging down a cliff to his death.

Comments: Doctor X was Wray's first of five horror films, and the first of three horror films directed by Michael Curtiz (*The Adventures of Robin Hood* and *Casablanca*), the other two being *Mystery of the Wax Museum* (again with Wray) and *The Walking Dead* (with Boris Karloff). Filmed in both Technicolor and black-and-white versions, with the more expensive Technicolor prints reserved for major engagements and the black-and-white prints used for small town exhibition and overseas distribution, *Doctor X* was shown only in black-and-white for decades until a surviving Technicolor print was rediscovered in the 1970s and released on video in the 1980s. A comparison of the two versions is fascinating, since there are slight variations of camera angle, and even minor differences (as

Part II. Sound Films

Doctor X **frame enlargement**

well as occasional flubs) in the dialogue. The color version, made to complete a contractual obligation with Technicolor, is the superior of the two, with better camera angles and the color photography exploiting designer Anton Grot's expressionistic sets to better advantage. Riding the crest of a horror movie craze initiated by Universal's *Dracula* and *Frankenstein* the year before, Warners–First National based *Doctor X* on the play *The Terror*, for which they paid $5,000. Wray gives one of her most appealing performances in *Doctor X,* in a lively, breathless and super-sexy turn that marked a departure from her previously demure manner in films, and almost seems like a preview of her *King Kong* role. On August 9, *Variety* commented on Wray: "Audiences won't recognize Fay Wray, unless they've seen her lately. She is a greatly changed personality but for the better."

Recalling *Doctor X*, Wray told co-author Roy Kinnard: "I did see *Doctor X* in preview [in 1932], but at that point I was not liking anything I was in very much because they were stereotypical roles, nothing very human about it, and I felt stuck in those things. I saw *Doctor X* [again] in Minneapolis just a couple of years ago [in 1989]. I thought it was paced a little too fast, that would be my criticism of it. But that didn't seem to bother the audience — they were pretty fascinated. I didn't have many personal conversations with Lee Tracy, but he was just like you see him on screen — kind of casual, easygoing and very snappy." Although Michael Curtiz did not have the light directorial touch of Universal's James Whale (*Frankenstein*), and lacked Whale's refined taste, he was one of Hollywood's top filmmakers, a zealous technician with real visual flair. Curtiz's handling of *Doctor X*, with the script's almost grisly emphasis on murder, cannibalism and deformity, is fascinating, and today the film seems almost like an unintended transition point between the restrained black-and-white horror movies of Universal and the more explicit color horror movies produced by Hammer Films decades later.

The Most Dangerous Game

RKO Radio, 1932; *Released:* September 16, 1932; *Executive Producer:* David O. Selznick; *Associate Producer:* Merian C. Cooper; *Directors:* Ernest B. Schoedsack,

Opposite: The Most Dangerous Game. Above: The Most Dangerous Game: With Joel McCrea; *bottom:* With Leslie Banks (*left, in black*), Noble Johnson (*center*) and Joel McCrea

***The Most Dangerous Game*:** With Joel McCrea (*top*) and Leslie Banks

Irving Pichel; *Screenplay:* James Ashmore Creelman, Based on the short story by Richard Connell; *Photography:* Henry Gerrard; *Camera Operators:* Russell Metty, Robert DeGrasse; *Assistant Cameraman:* Willard Barth; *Art Director:* Carroll Clark; *Set Decorator:* Thomas Little; *Film Editor:* Archie F. Marshek; *Music:* Max

Part II. Sound Films

***The Most Dangerous Game*:** With Joel McCrea

Steiner, Piano solos by Norma Boleslawski; *Sound Engineer:* Clem Portman; *Photographic Effects:* Lloyd Knechtel, Vernon L. Walker; *Optical Effects:* Linwood G. Dunn; *Art Technicians:* Mario Larrinaga, Byron L. Crabbe, *Special Effects:* Harry Redmond; *Miniatures:* Don Jahraus, Orville Goldner; *Special Props:* Marcel Delgado, John Cerisoli; *Costumes:* Walter Plunkett; *Still Photographer:* Gaston Longet (63 minutes)

Part II. Sound Films

Cast: Joel McCrea (Bob Rainsford), Fay Wray (Eve Trowbridge), Robert Armstrong (Martin Trowbridge), Leslie Banks (Count Zaroff), Noble Johnson (Ivan), Steve Clemento (Tartar), William Davidson (Captain), Landers Stevens (Doc), James Flavin (First Mate), Larry "Buster" Crabbe (Stunts)

Synopsis: Famed big game hunter Bob Rainsford is stranded on a remote tropical island when the yacht he has been aboard runs aground on coral reefs. Sole survivor Rainsford explores the island and discovers an imposing fortress inhabited by the Russian Count Zaroff and his servants.

Zaroff, also a professional hunter, recognizes Rainsford and welcomes him as a guest, introducing him to Martin Trowbridge and his sister Eve (FW), two other guests stranded from a previous shipwreck. Eve tries to warn Rainsford of impending danger as they socialize with the Count, and Rainsford gradually realizes that Zaroff is insane. Zaroff has caused the shipwrecks by shifting buoy lights marking the reefs; previous "guests" on the island were hunted down like animals by their sadistic host. Zaroff murders Eve's brother Martin and releases Eve and Rainsford into the jungle so that he can hunt them for sport. After an intense chase across the fog-shrouded island, Bob is apparently killed and Eve is recaptured by Zaroff. Rainsford, who faked his death, returns to the fortress and confronts Zaroff. After a violent and harrowing struggle with the madman, Rainsford overpowers Zaroff and escapes with Eve in a motorboat. Zaroff is preparing to shoot at them with a bow and arrow from a window but weakly falls from the window instead, into the pen of his own vicious hunting dogs.

Comments: This was the first and the best screen version of Richard Connell's thrilling story. Made for $218,869 and shot in four weeks during May and June of 1932, *The Most Dangerous Game* was a virtual dry run for *King Kong*, sharing many of its cast members, production personnel and sets with *Kong*. In fact, one of the reasons *The Most Dangerous Game* was produced was to minimize *King Kong*'s production cost; the huge jungle sets were charged off against *Game*'s budget instead of *Kong*'s. *The Most Dangerous Game* remains a thrilling film today, and stands as textbook example of editing technique — there is hardly a wasted shot in its tightly paced 63 minutes. The industry trade publication *Motion Picture Herald* listed this film's running time at 78 minutes based on preview screenings; if this is accurate, the movie was recut drastically, losing 15 minutes before release.

In a 1981 interview with co-author Roy Kinnard, Olympic swimming champion (and *Flash Gordon* serial star) Larry "Buster" Crabbe recalled performing some of the water stunts, doubling for Joel McCrea and others in the opening shipwreck scene.

Part II. Sound Films

The Most Dangerous Game was given a limited reissue in the late 1930s under the title *Skull Island*. In a 1993 interview with Roy Kinnard, Wray recalled, "I thought it was a very interesting story, with a wonderfully ironic twist — that humans should hunt each other instead of animals. Merian Cooper always had a different concept of making films, and I trusted him." Other film versions of Connell's short story have included *A Game of Death* (RKO, 1945), directed by *Citizen Kane* editor Robert Wise and using many stock shots from the 1932 original. The film starred John Loder and Audrey Long. Another major version was *Run for the Sun* (United Artists, 1956), starring Richard Widmark and Jane Greer, directed by Roy Boulting. There was also a tacky 1960s effort, *Bloodlust!*, and a made-for-TV movie starring Andy Griffith as the Zaroff character.

The Vampire Bat

Majestic, 1933; *Released:* January 21, 1933; *Producer:* Phil Goldstone; *Director:* Frank Strayer; *Screenplay:* Edward T. Lowe; *Photography:* Ira Morgan; *Art Director:* Daniel Hall; *Film Editor:* Otis Garrett; *Sound Engineer:* Dick Tyler (63 minutes)

Cast: Lionel Atwill (Dr. Otto von Niemann), Fay Wray (Ruth Bertin), Melvyn Douglas (Inspector Karl Brettschneider), Maude Eburne (Gussie Schnappmann), George E. Stone (Kringen), Dwight Frye (Herman Gleib), Robert Frazer (Emil Borst), Rita Carlisle (Martha Mueller), Lionel Belmore (Gustav Schoen), William V. Mong (Sauer), Stella Adams (Georgianna), Harrison Greene (Weingarten), Paul Weigel (Holdstadt), William Humphrey (Haupt), Fern Emmett (Gertrude), Carl Stockdale (Schmidt)

Synopsis: A series of grisly murders in the European village of Kleinschloss are attributed to vampirism, and Inspector Karl Brettschneider looks into the killings. Brettschneider is in love with Ruth Bertin (FW), assistant to Dr. Otto von Niemann, who confers with Brettschneider about the murders, offering various theories that might explain the mystery. Herman Gleib, a village idiot, is suspected, and the townspeople form a mob and hunt him down. Gleib dies when he flees into a cave and plunges into a crevice; he is found to have been innocent, though, when another murder occurs after his death. Brettschneider discovers that the murders were actually committed by Dr. von Niemann, who hypnotizes Emil, a servant, and telepathically orders him to kill. Ruth also discovers von Niemann's guilt; he tells her that he needed the victims' blood to endow artificial tissue he has created with life. He ties up Ruth and is about to drain her blood when he is surprised by Brettschneider and Emil. When Emil learns that he has unknowingly killed the victims under von Niemann's mental control, he shoots von Niemann and commits suicide. Brettschneider frees Ruth.

Comments: The Vampire Bat was produced during the apex of Hollywood's 1930s horror movie cycle, and almost succeeds in equaling Universal's product. Producer Phil Goldstone assembled a top-notch cast, and the film benefits greatly from being shot on sets rented from Universal. But Goldstone neglected to

*Top: **The Vampire Bat** portrait; bottom: **The Vampire Bat:** With Lionel Atwill and Maude Eburne*

Part II. Sound Films

The Vampire Bat: With Lionel Atwill

commission a good script; the hackneyed screenplay is the movie's weak point. Although there is certainly a mad scientist (Lionel Atwill) in *The Vampire Bat*, there is no titular vampire, and the film plays more or less like a pastiche of previous horror efforts. Nevertheless, the cast is an enjoyable one, with Dwight Frye imitating his *Dracula* role, complete with maniacal laugh. The technical credits are also first-rate, with bright, sharp photography by Ira Morgan. *The Vampire Bat* eventually became a reissue perennial, re-released by companies like Astor throughout the 1940s, and even playing into the 1950s under lurid alternate titles like *Forced to Sin* and *Blood Sucker*. A re-cut version, running a scant 45 minutes, has also been distributed. In 1993, Fay Wray told co-author Kinnard of *The Vampire Bat*: "I haven't seen [it]. I've heard some people say that it's just an awful film, and I've heard other people say it's very interesting, so I'm just going to let people argue over that. I'm not going to get involved." Oddly enough, Wray doesn't even scream in this horror film — not even once!

Part II. Sound Films

Mystery of the Wax Museum

Warner Bros., 1933; *Released:* February 18, 1933; *Director:* Michael Curtiz; *Screenplay:* Don Mullaly, Carl Erickson; *Story:* Charles S. Belden; *Photography (Technicolor):* Ray Rennahan; *Second Cameraman:* Roy Musgrave; *Assistant Cameramen:* Sam Brooks, Floyd Lee; *Art Director:* Anton Grot; *Film Editor:* George Amy; *Gowns:* Orry-Kelly; *Sound:* E. A. Brown; *Chief Electrician:* Claude Hutchinson; *Chief Grip:* Chuck Davis; *Props:* Limey Plews; *Still Photographer:* Scotty Welbourne; *Assistant Directors:* Frank Shaw, Lee Katz (78 minutes)

Cast: Lionel Atwill (Ivan Igor), Fay Wray (Charlotte Duncan), Glenda Farrell (Florence), Frank McHugh (Editor), Allen Vincent (Ralph Burton), Gavin Gordon (George Winton), Edwin Maxwell (Joe Worth), Holmes Herbert (Dr. Rasmussen), Claude King (Golatily), Arthur Edmund Carewe (Sparrow), Thomas Jackson (Detective), DeWitt Jennings (Captain of Police), Matthew Betz (Hugo), Monica Bannister (Joan Gale), Pat O'Malley (Plainclothesman), Bull Anderson (Janitor)

Synopsis: Ivan Igor, an accomplished sculptor, is trapped inside his wax museum in London when it is burned for the insurance money by Joe Worth, Igor's crooked partner.

Igor, now confined to a wheelchair, reopens the business in New York 12 years later. He is investigated by Florence, a newspaper reporter, when she notices that several figures in Igor's new museum resemble murder victims whose corpses were stolen.

Florence's roommate, Charlotte Duncan (FW), visits her fiancé Ralph, Igor's assistant, at the museum. When Igor meets Charlotte he is struck by her resemblance to a wax figure of Marie Antoinette destroyed in the London museum fire.

Florence discovers that the "sculptures" in Igor's museum are actually corpses coated with wax. The obsessed Igor, seeing an opportunity to restore his lost masterwork, lures Charlotte to his museum, planning to kill her and exhibit her corpse as the figure of Marie Antoinette. Attempting to escape, Charlotte struggles with Igor and accidentally shatters his "face," which had actually been a wax mask used to conceal his monstrous features, burned in the London fire. She is about to be encased in wax when Florence and Ralph arrive with policemen and rescue her. Battling with the policemen, Igor is killed when he falls into a vat of boiling wax.

Comments: Mystery of the Wax Museum was thought lost for many years, until a slightly worn print was discovered in 1970 and recopied as a joint venture

Mystery of the Wax Museum pre-release ad

between the American Film Institute and United Artists, the film's distributor at that time. Better, and far superior prints of the film were later made, and released on video, when ownership passed to Ted Turner. One of the most well-regarded and memorable horror films produced in the 1930s, *Mystery* has many notewor-

Top: Mystery of the Wax Museum; bottom: A lobby card from *Mystery of the Wax Museum:* with Glenda Farrell (*right*)

Mystery of the Wax Museum: With Lionel Atwill

thy scenes, chief among them the justifiably famed "unmasking" scene, in which a terrified Wray shatters Atwill's face, really a waxen disguise covering his deformed face. Well-directed by Michael Curtiz, the film bears many similarities to his previous *Doctor X*, but makes far better use of Technicolor in general design and overall effect. An unambitious but well-mounted little film, *Mystery of the Wax Museum* is justifiably revered as a genre classic.

Discussing the film with Kinnard in 1993, Wray recalled: "Lionel Atwill was a very professional person, very proper ... *Mystery of the Wax Museum* had certain strengths. Originally, it was very harsh color-wise. Then I saw the film recently, restored by UCLA, and I thought they did a *beautiful* job. The color had a kind of antique look that took away the harshness I remember when I saw it in preview.... The colors in the restoration were very mellow, and it was fascinating, The problem at that time with color was that they needed so much light in order to photograph that it was just devastating. It was really, really hot, and that was tough.

"On *Wax Museum*, Glenda Farrell was very talkative, had a lot of energy, was full of good spirits and was just a very enthusiastic, energetic, competent

Part II. Sound Films

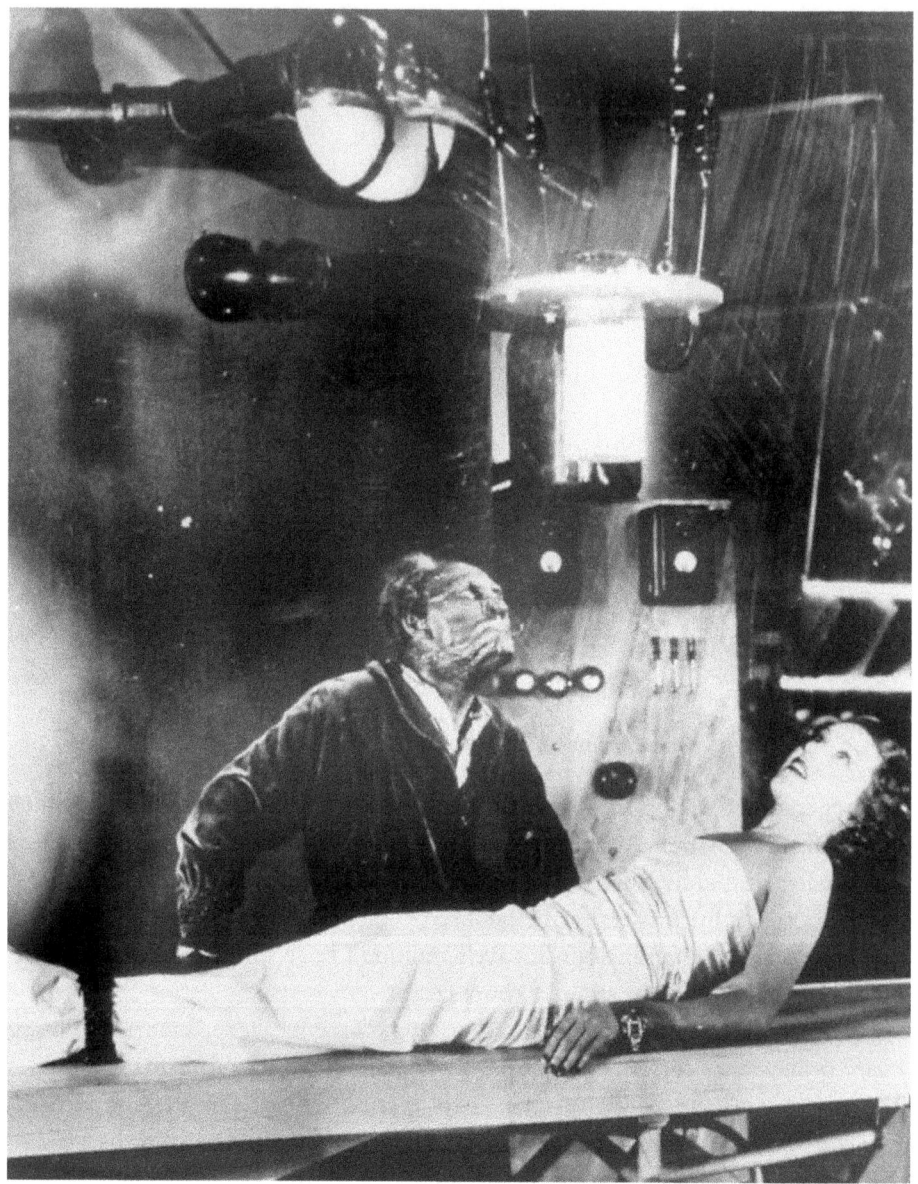

***Mystery of the Wax Museum*:** With Lionel Atwill

actress. She was a comedic type, and I thought she was very clever in that direction. She was smooth and very good.

"I really didn't know Lionel Atwill well. I made three films with him, but we never had an extended conversation. He was polite enough, but seemed more interested in checking to see if his profile was correct.

"Michael Curtiz — well, he was a very able director, very efficient, but very unemotional, almost like a machine. He didn't give detailed direction; you just knew the scene had to be done, and so you do it.

"In the unmasking scene for *Mystery of the Wax Museum*, they only had two masks, so they could only film the scene twice. I wasn't allowed to see Atwill's makeup before the scene was shot, and when I first cracked the mask and saw that makeup, I stopped and backed away, which is what I felt a real person would actually do. But Curtiz wanted me to break away the entire mask and ordered the scene reshot."

Her memories appear to be accurate judging from the film itself, as Curtiz seems to have used portions of both takes in the final edit.

Mystery of the Wax Museum was filmed under the title *Wax Museum*, and some publicity materials, as well as the countdown leaders of the film itself, still carried that title at the time of release.

Mystery of the Wax Museum was remade by Warner Bros. in 1953 as *House of Wax*, starring Vincent Price and Phyllis Kirk. The film was directed in color and 3-D by Andre de Toth. Although it was an enjoyable picture, *House of Wax* lacked the careful attention to detail and the overall conviction of the Curtiz original. A 1960s TV series based on the general concept was planned but then dropped; the pilot episode was theatrically exhibited under the title *Chamber of Horrors* in 1966. Elements of the story have also turned up in horror films like *A Bucket of Blood* and *Track of the Vampire*, among others.

Below the Sea

Columbia, 1933; *Released:* March 29, 1933; *Director:* Albert Rogell; *Story and Screenplay:* Jo Swerling; *Photography:* Joseph Walker; *Film Editor:* Jack Dennis; *Sound:* George Cooper; *Undersea Technician:* E. Roy Davidson (79 minutes)

Cast: Ralph Bellamy (Steve "Mac" McCreary), Fay Wray (Diana Templeton), Fredrick Vogeding (Capt. von Boulten/Karl Schlemmer), Esther Howard (Lily), Paul Page (Burt Jackson), Trevor Bland (Horace Waldridge), William J. Kelly (Dr. Chapman), Richard Alexander (Sailor), Kenneth MacDonald, Paul McVey

Synopsis: In World War I, a German U-boat commanded by Capt. von Boulten is transporting a $3,000,000 gold shipment when the sub is sunk by a British ship. Von Boulten and his lieutenant survive and swim ashore; von Boulten then murders the lieutenant, keeping a map showing the location of the sub's wreckage.

Twelve years later, von Boulten, using the alias Karl Schlemmer, teams up with diver Steve McCreary and they travel to the treasure site with Lily, who has financed the expedition, planning to split the salvaged gold three ways. Their scheme fails, though, when their crew nearly mutinies and their ship is sunk in a storm. Steve, distrustful of Schlemmer, tears the treasure map in half and keeps part of it himself, thereby guaranteeing their partnership in any future effort to recover the gold. Three years later, socialite Diana Templeton (FW) finances an oceanographic expedition which McCreary and Schlemmer join. Steve and Diana become romantically involved. When Steve and Schlemmer attempt to salvage the U-boat treasure again, Diana is trapped in a diving bell that is attacked by a giant octopus. Steve rescues Diana in his diving suit, but Schlemmer loses the treasure a third time when the container holding it breaks as it is being raised to the surface. The gold spills into the sea, dragging Schlemmer with it as his foot is entangled in a chain. All chance of recovering the treasure is now lost forever.

Below the Sea: **Columbia Pictures portrait**

Comments: Shot in only three weeks, *Below the Sea* looks better than its low budget and short production schedule might indicate, largely due to the expert lens work of cinematographer Joseph Walker. Although the film is available and has been shown on cable television, current prints are incomplete, missing a color sequence (running three or four minutes), depicting undersea animal life, that

Top: ***Below the Sea****; bottom:* ***Below the Sea:*** with Ralph Bellamy

Below the Sea

is screened at a fund-raising dinner. Wray, looking great in this film, had apparently been pursued by so many movie monsters up to this point that the filmmakers couldn't resist placing her in further jeopardy; at one point, trapped in a submerged diving bell, she is attacked by a giant octopus!

Part II. Sound Films

King Kong

RKO-Radio, 1933; *Released:* April 7, 1933; *Producer:* David O. Selznick; *Directors:* Merian C. Cooper, Ernest B. Schoedsack; *Screenplay:* James Creelman, Ruth Rose; *Scenario Associate:* Horace McCoy; *Photography:* Eddie Linden, Vernon Walker, J. O. Taylor; *Camera Operators:* Edward Henderson, Felix Schoedsack, Lee Davis; *Assistant Cameramen:* Bert Willis, William Reinhold, William Clothier, Clifford Stine; *Optical Photography:* William Ulm; *Rear Projection Process:* Sidney Saunders; *Dunning Matte Process Supervisors:* Carroll C. Dunning, C. Dodge Dunning, *Williams Matte Process Supervisor:* Frank Williams; *Special Effects Chief Technician:* Willis H. O'Brien; *Technical Staff:* E. B. Gibson, Marcel Delgado, Fred Reese, Orville Goldner, Carroll Shepphird; *Art Technicians:* Mario Larrinaga, Byron L. Crabbe; *Art Technicians:* Mario Larrinaga, Byron L. Crabbe; *Technical Artists:* Victor Delgado, Zachary Hoag, Juan Larrinaga; *Sculptor:* John Cerisoli; *Painting Technician:* Peter Stitch; *Film Editor:* Ted Cheesman; *Sound Effects:* Murray Spivack; *Sound Recordist:* Earl A. Wolcott; *Supervising Art Director:* Van Nest Polglase; *Sets:* Carroll Clark, Al Herman; *Set Decorator:* Thomas Little; *Construction Technician:* W. G. White; *Makeup Supervisor:* Mel Berns, *Costumes:* Walter Plunkett; *Additional Costumes:* Western Costume Co.; *Additional Special Effects:* Harry Redmond, Jr.; *Production Assistants:* Archie F. Marshek, Walter Daniels; *Camera Airplane Pilots:* Duke Krantz, George Weiss; *Assistant Directors:* Ivan Thomas, Doran Cox, Walter Daniels, Assistant to Merian C. Cooper: Zoe Porter; *Technical Advisors:* Dr. J. W. Lytle, Dr. O. A. Patterson, Dr. Harry C. Raven; *Art Titles:* Pacific Title Co. (100 minutes)

Cast: Fay Wray (Ann Darrow), Robert Armstrong (Carl Denham), Bruce Cabot (Jack Driscoll), Frank Reicher (Capt. Englehorn), Sam Hardy (Charles Weston), Noble Johnson (Native Chief), Steve Clemento (Witch King), James Flavin (Second Mate), Victor Wong (Charlie), Dick Curtis, Fred Behrle, Earl "Hap" Hogan, Walter Kirby, John Northpole, H. R. Warwick, Jack Gallagher, Duke Green, Jockey Haefeli, Sam Levine, Sailor Vincent, Kid Wagner, Charles Hall, George Magrill, Van Alder, John Collins, Charles Sewell, Bill Van Vleck, Ralph Bard, T. C. Jacks, Harry Claremont, Art Flavin, Walter Kimpton, Richie McCarew, Jack Perry, Bert O'Malley, Jack Silver, Joe Dill, Leo Beard, Jimmy Dime, Tex Duffy, Shorty English, Bill Fisher, Ethan Laidlaw, Hugh Starkey, Bill Dagwell, Roy Brent, Larry Fisher, Walter Taylor, Skeets Noyes, Edward Clark, Blackie Whiteford, Jack Saunders, Harry Walker, Frank Gerrity, Harry Cornbleth, Bud Mason, Charles Sullivan, Al McDonald, James Casey (*Venture* Crew Members),

Top left and right: King Kong: Studio portraits; *bottom: King Kong* scene

Part II. Sound Films

King Kong

Tex Higginson (Crewman/Taxi Driver), John Crawford, Nim Nixon, Edward Patrick, T. J. Rankin, Gus Robinson, Jim Thorpe (Native Dancers), Everett Brown (Native in Ape Costume), John Wade, Milton Shockley, John Brakins, Sam Marlowe, Ivory Williams, Tobias Tally, Al Knight, Charles Washington, William

Top: King Kong: A studio artist's conception of the notorious censored scene. *Bottom: King Kong*

Part II. Sound Films

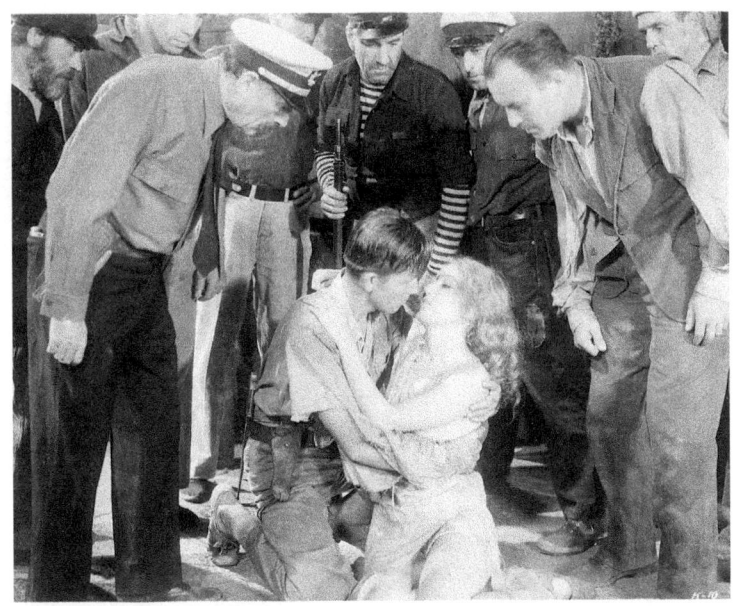

Top: King Kong: With Frank Reicher, Bruce Cabot and Robert Armstrong; *bottom: King Kong*: With Bruce Cabot and Robert Armstrong (in dress clothes)

Part II. Sound Films

***King Kong*:** **With director Ernest B. Schoedsack**

Duran, Henry Martin, Floyd Shackelford, Johnnie Bland, Jack Best, George Washington, Cliff Ingram, Roy Thompskin, Earl Turman, Blue Washington, Odel Conley, Onest Conley, John Davis (Native Warriors), Wade Walker, William Dunn, Ed Allen, A. J. Prather, Walter Knox, Ray Turner, Jack West, Tom Shelly, Nathan Perry, Alice Nichols, Katherine Curry, Annie L. Jackson, Evelyn Garrison, Etta Mae Allen, Rose Dandridge, Etta Mae Henry, Joe Flourney, Ameta Muse, Fanny Donahue, Lawrence Green, William Solder, Katherine Sparks, Etta McDaniel (Natives), Hannah Washington, James Adamson, Bernice Dandridge, Rena Marlowe, Malcolm Potts, Harold Garrison (Native Children), Irene Henry (Native Baby), Madame Sul-te-wan (Native Handmaiden), Sandra Shaw (Hotel Victim), Russ Powell (Dock Watchman), Bill Nye, George McQuarrie (Police Captains), Frank Fanning, Monte Vandegrift, Frank Meredith (Police Officers), Tom Lonergan (Police Officer/Usher), Allen Pomeroy (Motorcycle Policeman), Ivan Thomas (Conductor), Joe Marba (Motorman), George Daly (Machine Gun-

Part II. Sound Films

King Kong publicity poses

King Kong publicity poses

Part II. Sound Films

***King Kong*:** With Robert Armstrong

ner), Lew Harvey, Pat Harmon (Gunmen), Paul Porcasi (Street Vendor), Eddie Sturgis, King Mojave, Harry Eaton, Mae Marrin, Larry McGrath (Ballyhooers), Jack Pratt (Radio Announcer), Eddie Boland, Lynton Brent, Paddy O'Flynn, Syd Saylor (Reporters/Cameramen), Frank Mills, Frank O'Connor, Russ Saunders, Harry Bowen, Eddie Hart, Peter Duray, Wesley Hopper, Roy Stewart, Charles

Part II. Sound Films

King Kong: With Bruce Cabot

O'Malley, Jack Smith, Ed Stevens, Ed Reed, Ed Rochelle, Jack Chapin, Harry Mount, Ralph Easton, Frank Cullen, Frank Angel, Walt Ackerman, Arnold Gray (Reporters), James Harrison, Lee Phelps (Cameramen), Jean Fenwick, Hazel Howell, Betty Gale, Bill Williams, LeRoy Mason (New Yorkers), Larry Steers, Earl

King Kong: A promotional ad with Bruce Cabot for Borden's Milk

Dwire (Theatergoers), June Gittelson (Fat Woman), Vera Lewis (Dowager), Oliver Eckhardt (Husband), Walter Downing, John L. Johnson, Harry Duvall, Gertrude Sutton, Helen Worthington, Jean Doran, Florence Dudley, Betty Burns, Tom O'Grady, Harry Strang, Lillian Young, Dorothy Gulliver, Carlotta Monti (Bits), Reginald Barlow (Engineer), Barney Capehart, Bob Galloway, Eric Wood, Rusty Mitchell, Russ Rogers (Pilots), Merian C. Cooper, Ernest B. Schoedsack (Pilots), Jame Casey, Tex Higginson (Stunt Doubles), Aline Goodwin, Pauline Wagner, Lee Kinney, Lillian Jones, Marcella Allen, Cherie May (Fay Wray Stunt Doubles), Charles Sullivan, Bob McKee, Mike Lally, Bob Williams (Robert Armstrong Stunt Doubles), Al McDonald, Gil Perkins (Bruce Cabot Stunt Doubles), Bud Mason (James Flavin Stunt Double), Mike Graves (Stunt Double on Log), Sam Cummings, Edith Haskins, Billy Jones, Chic Collins, Johnny St. Claire, Jack Holbrook, Betty Collins, Loretta Rush, Bobby Rose, Frances Mills (Stunt Doubles), Harvey Perry (Crash Stunt)

Synopsis: Documentary film producer Carl Denham sets sail for uncharted Skull Island in the Indian Ocean to shoot a new movie, and hires an unemployed film extra, Ann Darrow (FW), to lend romantic interest to the movie. Ann falls in love with first mate Jack Driscoll en route to the island.

When the expedition finally arrives on Skull Island, they are confronted by savage tribesmen who want to sacrifice Ann to their god Kong, an omnipotent deity living in the jungles beyond an enormous wall. Denham and his men retreat to the ship with Ann, but she is kidnapped by the tribe that night, taken to the island and tied to a sacrificial altar, where she is claimed by Kong, a gigantic ape who carries her away into the jungle.

Denham, Jack Driscoll and the ship's crew follow in an attempt to rescue Ann. Most of them are killed when they are attacked by Kong and various prehistoric beasts living on the island, but Denham escapes and returns to the beach. Driscoll manages to rescue Ann from Kong and rejoin them on the other side of the wall.

The enraged Kong follows, crashing through the gates of the huge wall and destroying the village. The rampaging monster is subdued by a powerful gas bomb hurled by Denham, and the beast collapses unconscious. Seeing a money-making opportunity, Denham transports him to New York, where the huge ape is placed on exhibition in a theater. Kong escapes and recaptures Ann, climbing the Empire State Building with her in his grasp. At the pinnacle of the building, Kong gently places Ann on a ledge out of harm's way as he is attacked by planes armed with machine-guns. Mortally wounded, he plunges to his doom as Driscoll arrives to rescue Ann.

Part II. Sound Films

Comments: More than 70 years after its release, there are few people unfamiliar with the basic plot of *King Kong*, the beauty-and-the beast fantasy of a giant gorilla entranced by a blonde, captured on a lost island by a movie producer, and brought back to civilization only to meet his doom atop the Empire State Building. There are few movies that have been able to match the longevity and continuing popularity of *King Kong*. The creation of producer Merian C. Cooper, who co-directed with his long-time partner Ernest B. Schoedsack (together they filmed the great silent documentaries *Grass* and *Chang*, as well *The Four Feathers*), *King Kong* was in production for over a year, costing $678,000 at a time when the average studio film was budgeted at $200,000. On release, the film proved immediately beneficial to financially ailing RKO-Radio, grossing $2,000,000 for the studio in the darkest days of the Great Depression and becoming one of the highest grossing movies of the 30s. It was reissued nationally six times by RKO (the 1952 re-release, the first to be promoted with television ads, was especially successful, with a $3,000,000 box office take), and reissued again on a limited basis by Janus Films in the early 1970s. The film has also demonstrated its enduring popularity in television syndication and on home video. More than just a great fantasy movie, *King Kong* transcends its genre and stands today as one of the greatest movies of *any* type ever produced.

Conceived by Merian C. Cooper, *King Kong* could hardly have been realized without the artistry and technical expertise of special effects genius Willis H. O'Brien — and O'Brien definitely *was*, to use that clichéd Hollywood term, a genius. With *King Kong*, O'Brien's meticulous frame-by-frame stop-motion puppet animation, previously on display in First National's silent dinosaur thriller *The Lost World* (1925), grew to full maturity. Basing his pictorial design on the eerie black-and-white illustrations of Gustave Doré, O'Brien and his crew brought forth an alien, strangely beautiful prehistoric landscape on the uncharted island inhabited by Kong, the huge ape and other prehistoric monsters animated with a degree of power and vitality unattained before and seldom equaled since, even in the color stop-motion fantasies of Ray Harryhausen. Incredibly, only eight years separate *The Lost World* from *King Kong*; without minimizing *The Lost World* (a groundbreaking film in its own right), the two films seem light years apart technically. Constructed on a relatively large scale (the brontosaurus figure was several feet in length), the *King Kong* animation puppets, beautifully crafted by O'Brien's associate Marcel Delgado, had great textural detail, the size of the models allowing flexibility and subtlety in lighting and photography.

In addition to the time-consuming stop-motion animation, a variety of other special effects were used to give Merian Cooper's vision life, including rear projection, optical mattes, double exposure, full-scale mock-ups and miniature projection (used to insert live actors into scale model sets). Few of these techniques were new, but never before had they been employed in combination with such vigor and imagination. Enhancing it all was Max Steiner's throbbing, powerful original music score, one of the earliest — and best — ever composed for a movie. *King Kong* was the *Star Wars* of its day, redefining its own genre as it expanded cinematic technique, as well as redefining audience perceptions and expectations.

King Kong, though, was more than just a special effects "popcorn" movie; the film's mythic approach and surreal, nightmare imagery elevate it to a higher artistic plane than any of its successors or imitators. If special effects were all that *King Kong* had to offer, it would have been forgotten years ago, as many of its lesser offshoots have been, remembered only by film buffs. Instead, the movie, as one historian has said, "is now folklore," outlasting its more prestigious, award-winning contemporaries. Hollywood production technology has advanced, leaving hand-made films like *Kong* in its digital wake, but the passage of time has also thrown the movie's other, previously neglected qualities into sharper relief.

King Kong is one of the few movies of its type with a human cast that refuses to be dominated by overwhelming special effects, and a good deal of *Kong's* impact is due to the iconoclastic performance — and near-nudity — of top-billed Fay Wray. It's an *unreal* performance, breathless, wide-eyed and essentially innocent, almost a fan-magazine view of what the aspiring young actress she plays would be like. Twenty-five when her scenes were being shot in late 1932, Wray was at the height of her beauty, meticulously photographed here with light makeup and a flowing blonde wig. The wholesome sex appeal she projects is remarkably similar to Marilyn Monroe's screen persona in movies like *The Seven Year Itch,* and one wonders if a young Monroe could possibly have seen Wray in *King Kong*. Although there is never anything objectionable or indecent about her performance in *Kong,* Wray certainly displays plenty of exposed anatomy in the studio publicity photos; although tame by modern standards, her frequent state of undress in the film and advertising stills must have raised a few eyebrows at the time. Some footage of the scantily clad actress *did* cause problems with the censors, most notably a scene in which Wray is disrobed and tickled by Kong. Although considered acceptable on the film's original 1933 release, this scene was cut and suppressed on reissue in 1938 and was thought lost until a print of the sequence, as well as other cut scenes involving violence perpetrated by Kong, were rediscovered and restored in the 1970s. Another potentially objectionable scene of Wray has *always* been in the film, even when it has been shown on television: After being rescued from Kong by Bruce Cabot, they escape by diving into a lake and for a moment Wray's breast is fully exposed. The shot was never cut or censored on TV, perhaps because of its brevity in this quickly paced scene. Censored or not, though, *King Kong* owes a lot to Fay Wray, and she made *King Kong* one of the few "monster on the loose" movies with real sex appeal.

In 1993, Wray recalled *King Kong* for co-author Roy Kinnard: "The first time I saw *King Kong* I was distressed by how much screaming there was in it — it seemed too much to me, and I realized only later that a lot of screaming was necessary in order to give life to the little animated figure of me in Kong's hand, and without the screaming, it *wouldn't* have seemed alive. These essentially had to be long shots, but still, *all* of that screaming seemed overdone to me at the time.

"Merian Cooper was one of the most unusual men ever to work in films, and he was one of the most unusual characters in my life. He had a background that was astonishing. Born in Florida, he was a real 'Southern Gentleman,' and had a chivalrous attitude toward women. He had graduated from a Naval academy, and after he left the Navy, he decided to become a journalist. During the First World War, Cooper went to Persia. He was shot down and taken prisoner by the Russians, but then escaped. He met Ernest Schoedsack, who was driving an ambulance. They met on a station platform and they just hit it off, became good friends — and that's when they went off to make pictures together in faraway places. Pretty colorful, right? Cooper liked the wilderness and animals, and yet was a very intelligent, social person. But he really liked faraway places better than civilization. He was fascinating; I looked upon him as a kind of father figure. I enjoyed knowing him, always, and I thought he was one of my very best friends."

Wray said that the question she was most often asked about *Kong* was "'How did they *do* it?,' 'Was that a big animal?,' 'Was that a man in a suit?,' and of course the answer to those questions is, 'No, that was an 18-inch tall figure.' Then the question follows, 'Well, how did they get pictures of you in an 18-inch tall figure's hand?,' and so I explain about the full-sized Kong hand, and how once I was secure in it, with the fingers pressed tightly around me, they photographed me quite separately from anything else. There were special problems just in the way it was done: having to imagine Kong instead of having anyone or anything to look at. That was a good thing, because you're allowed the freedom of your imagination, but it was tough in a way, too. I don't see it that way, though. It was a performance that I just did, and I don't think in terms of the difficulties.

"Bruce [Cabot] was fine. He was okay, very straightforward; Robert Armstrong, too, was very straightforward and *very* professional. [Willis O'Brien] came on the set one day, but didn't mingle. I just remember *seeing* him on the set. He was such a gifted man, I would have liked to have talked to him, but I didn't."

Asked if she had any indication at that time that *Kong* would become a film classic, Wray responded, "Of course not; whenever one makes a film, you want it to be good, but I don't think anyone ever predicts such a sustained life for a film. I really wasn't thinking that way at all. We couldn't have imagined that, and it's kind of wonderful that *King Kong* has endured. As time goes on, I feel so pleased that the film is really appreciated. I'm certain it has been shown in every country in the world, and that gives me a good feeling; I'm happy to know that it has had that broad reception. *King Kong* has had a lovely impact. I didn't realize for the first ten years after it was released *how much* it was appreciated, and then, as time goes by, *King Kong* seems to have even grown in appeal, so I am very glad — that just makes me feel good."

The inevitable sequel to *King Kong*, *The Son of Kong*, was rushed into production immediately after the release of the first movie. Robert Armstrong returned without Wray and Cabot; the picture was shot on less than half of its predecessor's budget. Although an enjoyable little film, it was eclipsed in the shadow of the original. Incredibly, it was produced with such economical speed that RKO had it in theaters *the same year* as *King Kong*!

A *King Kong* spin-off, dealing with a far gentler over-sized ape, was produced by Cooper in 1949. *Mighty Joe Young* was not a successful movie financially, but did earn a long-overdue Academy Award for Willis O'Brien. (Actually, about 85 percent of the film's model animation was actually done by O'Brien's assistant, Ray Harryhausen, who was then in the early stages of his career as a special effects artist.)

The character of King Kong was licensed for use in two foreign monster movies, *King Kong vs. Godzilla* (1963) and *King Kong Escapes* (1968), both produced in Japan. Although neither movie was in the same league as the original, these wide-screen color fantasies were targeted at a largely juvenile audience and, full of action, succeed on that level. Neither film employed Willis O'Brien's stop-motion animation, opting instead for the more expedient technique of costumed actors playing the monsters.

The same was true of *King Kong*, the 1976 Paramount remake, produced by Dino De Laurentiis, directed by John Guillermin and starring Jessica Lange. It was deceitfully publicized as being filmed with a technologically advanced robot appearing as Kong, but the much-ballyhooed mechanical wonder only appeared in a few brief shots, with makeup expert Rick Baker playing Kong in nearly every scene! Although not as horrendously bad as many of its detractors claimed, the film was certainly a letdown and a major disappointment, vastly inferior to the original and totally lacking that film's mythic appeal and sense of wonder.

As of this writing, a second *King Kong* remake, to be directed by Peter Jackson, has been announced for release in late 2005, but the 1933 original goes on, refusing to fade from the popular consciousness after more than 70 years. In analyzing this film's continuing appeal, the authors do not agree with those who claim that the film contains *hidden* racial, sexual, social and economic issues, other than what is apparent to the casual viewer. Cooper and everyone else connected with its making firmly denied that these notions were implied. *King Kong* was only intended to be exactly what it appears to be: a shrewdly formulated entertainment, calculated to draw an audience into its world of fantasy.

One of the film's more obvious — and most effective — assets is composer Max Steiner's music score. A good example of the score's artistry is to be heard in the final scene depicting Kong's death atop the Empire State Building. The music heard during this sequence uses the "Kong" and "Stolen Love" motifs heard earlier and throughout the film in its last two-thirds; however, it is only here that these two musical themes are finally intertwined and resolved, giving the audience an opportunity to recall the scenes they have viewed up to that point. When Kong looks at Ann for a final moment, then plunges from the Empire State Building in a fall that is almost suicidal, the music passionately builds in volume, recalling the (fictional) "Old Arabian Proverb" that opened the film: "And lo! The Beast looked upon the face of beauty. And it stayed its hand from killing. And from that day it was as one dead." Robert Armstrong's character Carl Denham never did make the movie that he had intended to film on Kong's island, but Merian C. Cooper certainly made his.

The Woman I Stole

Columbia, 1933; *Released:* May 1, 1933; *Director:* Irving Cummings; *Screenplay:* Jo Swerling, Based on the novel *Tampico* by Joseph Hergesheimer; *Photography:* Benjamin Kline; *Film Editor:* Gene Havlick; *Sound Engineer:* Edward Bernds; *Assistant Director:* David Selman (69 minutes)

Cast: Jack Holt (Jim Bradier), Fay Wray (Vida Corew), Noah Beery (Gen. Rayon), Raquel Torres (Teresita), Donald Cook (Stephen Corew), Edwin Maxwell

(Lentz), Charles Brown (Deleker), Ferdinand Munier (Sixto), Lee Phelps (Murdock)

Synopsis: After a prolonged absence, engineer Jim Bradier returns to North African oil fields he had formerly supervised with the intention of romancing Vida Corew (FW), the wife of Stephen Corew, who had been appointed general manager by Jim.

Vida is attracted to Jim, but their illicit romance is interrupted when the oil fields are sabotaged by Gen. Rayon, a bandit. Jim is about to claim Vida for himself in a confrontation with Stephen, but Stephen accuses him of having left the oil fields in the first place out of cowardice. To prove him wrong Jim decides to stay and team up with Stephen against Rayon.

Jim arranges a face-to-face meeting with Rayon, discovering to his surprise that the bandit is really working for Lentz, a dishonest business partner of Jim's who is scheming to take over the oil fields. Jim convinces Rayon to work for him instead, and is able to prove Lentz's complicity in the oil field raids to Stephen. Jim's feelings for Vida wane, and he rejects her because of her infidelity to Stephen, whom he now considers a friend. Jim leaves, boarding a ship bound for America, and is surprised to encounter Stephen, who has also left Vida. Together they toast their freedom.

Comments: This tale of adventure in the oil fields, laced with marital infidelity and marauding bandits, was filmed in three weeks during February and March of '33. Wray was cast somewhat against type as a faithless wife. The working title of the film was *Tampico*.

Ann Carver's Profession

Columbia, 1933; *Released:* May 26, 1933; *Director:* Eddie Buzzell; *Story and Screenplay:* Robert Riskin; *Photography:* Ted Tetzlaff; *Assistant Cameramen:* Jack Anderson, Al Keller; *Second Cameraman:* Andre Berlatier; *Film Editor:* Maurice Wright; *Gowns:* Letty Lee; *Sound Engineer:* Edward Bernds; *Assistant Director:* Sam Nelson (68 minutes)

Cast: Fay Wray (Ann Carver), Gene Raymond ("Lightning" Bill Graham), Claire Dodd (Carole Rogers), Jessie Ralph (Terry), Claude Gillingwater (Judge Bingham), Frank Albertson (Jim Thompson), Arthur Pierson (Ken), Frank Reicher (The General), George Baxter (Chedo), David Newell (Adjutant), Frank Conroy (Baker), Robert Barrat (Mr. Simmons), Edward Keane (Mr. Harrison), Diane Bori (Irma Chappelle)

Part II. Sound Films

Ann Carver's Profession: With Gene Raymond

Synopsis: College football star "Lightning" Bill Graham marries his sweetheart Ann Carver (FW). She has earned a law degree, but is content to be a housewife when Bill finds employment as a draftsman. Ann eventually begins to practice law, though, and becomes a successful attorney. The demands of Ann's legal career soon disrupt her marriage. Ashamed because his wife earns more than he does, Bill is disillusioned, and they begin to drift apart. Bill is pursued romantically by Carole Rogers, an alcoholic nightclub singer, who dies in a freak accident. He is wrongfully charged with murder and Ann defends him in court. She wins an acquittal after delivering an impassioned plea to the jury, convincing them that reasonable doubt exists, and they are reconciled.

Ann Carver's Profession

Comments: A somewhat improbable romantic drama, *Ann Carver's Profession* has a more enlightened view of its female protagonist than was common in most "women's pictures" of the time. The main flaw is that Wray is somewhat miscast; she lacks the aggressive personality the role calls for. This was noted by contemporary reviewers. *Ann Carver's Profession* was scripted by Robert Riskin, who would become Wray's second husband nine years later, and who was soon to begin a profitable association with top Columbia director Frank Capra. The higher quality of the *Ann Carver's* script aside, the film, and perhaps Wray as well, could have used the directorial guidance of a Capra; director Eddie Buzzell, a former stage comic and crony of Columbia founder and president Harry Cohn, was little more than an assembly-line hack. The movie was shot in less than three weeks during March and April of '33. The working titles were *Rules for Wives* (the title of Robert Riskin's original story) and *Professional Women*.

Part II. Sound Films

The Big Brain

RKO-Radio, 1933; *Released:* June 16, 1933; *Associate Producer:* Samuel Bischoff; *Director:* George Archainbaud, *Screenplay:* Sy Bartlett; *Continuity:* Warren B. Duff; *Photography:* Arthur Edeson; *Camera Operator:* Harry Davis; *Assistant Cameramen:* Bert Eason, Vernon Larson; *Art Director:* Ralph DeLacy; *Film Editor:* Rose Loewinger; *Supervising Film Editor:* Martin G. Cohn; *Editorial Assistant:* Stanley Kolbert; *Sound Recording:* Hans Weeren, Whitley Howett; *Recording Assistants:* Alf Burton, Gilbert Pollack, Martin Jackson; *Chief Electrician:* Al Cahen, Don Donaldson; *Chief Grip:* Robert Murphy; *Props:* Charles Henley; *Still Photography:* Roman Freulich; *Assistant Director:* Eric Stacey (72 minutes)

Cast: George E. Stone (Max Werner), Phillips Holmes (Terry Van Sloan), Fay Wray (Cynthia Glennon), Minna Gombell (Margy), Reginald Owen (Lord Darlington), Lillian Bond (Dorothy Norton), Reginald Mason (Lord Latham), Sam Hardy ("Slick" Ryan), Lucien Littlefield (Justice of the Peace), Douglass Dumbrille (Dan Thomas), Berton Churchill (Col. Higginbothom), Robert Emmett O'Connor (Detective), Edgar Norton (Butler), Charles McNaughton (Wallack), Lya Lys, Guy Usher, Claude King, Dell Henderson, C. Montague Shaw

Synopsis: Gambler Max Werner rises to prominence in the underworld, acquiring great wealth and influence through his shady business dealings in America and overseas. He is eventually ruined by his obsession with Cynthia Glennon (FW), a wealthy socialite who rejects his advances and then engineers Werner's capture by the authorities.

Comments: One of Wray's most potentially interesting 1930s films, *The Big Brain* remains unavailable, and may be lost. This gangster melodrama was produced by K. B. S. productions and released by RKO-Radio. It was reissued in the 1940s, but has since dropped out of sight, and was not included in the package of RKO titles released to television in the 1950s by C&C. The film's cast and technical credits are solid, and if nothing else, *The Big Brain* would certainly be good to *look* at — it was photographed by Arthur Edeson, one of Hollywood's best cinematographers (*Frankenstein, The Maltese Falcon, Casablanca*).

Shanghai Madness

Fox, 1933; *Released:* August 4, 1933; Producer: Al Rockett; *Supervising Producer:* Winfield R. Sheehan; *Director:* John Blystone; *Screenplay:* Austin Parker; Based

Part II. Sound Films

Shanghai Madness: **With Spencer Tracy and Eugene Pallette**

on the short story by Frederick Hazlitt Brennan, Adapted by Austin Parker and Gordon Wong Wellesley, with contributions by Edward T. Lowe; *Photography:* Lee Garmes; *Camera Operators:* John Schmitz, Stanley Cortez; *Assistant Cameramen:* Warner Cruz, H. C. Smith; *Film Editors:* Margaret Clancy, Alexander Troffey; *Gowns:* Rita Kaufman; *Music Director:* Louis De Francesco; *Sound:* W. W. Lindsay, Jr.; *Assistant Sound Engineer:* J. Sigler; *Unit Manager:* Ed Berry; *Still Photographer:* Emmett Schoenbaum; *Assistant Director:* Jasper Blystone (63 minutes)

Cast: Spencer Tracy (Lt. Patrick "Pat" H. Johnson), Fay Wray (Wildeth Christie), Ralph Morgan (Li Po Chang), Eugene Pallette (Capt. Lobo Lornegan), Herbert Mundin (Third Officer Jones), Reginald Mason (William Christie), Arthur Hoyt (Van Emery), Albert Conti (Rigaud), Maude Eburne (Mrs. Glissen), William von Brincken (Von Uhlemburg), Frederick Burton

Synopsis: Lt. Patrick H. Jackson is court-martialed and discharged from the Navy after he fires on a Communist-held fort in Shanghai. Jackson, resentful of his discharge and unable to find work in Shanghai as a result, befriends wealthy socialite Wildeth Christie (FW), after rescuing her from a riot. Jackson and

Wildeth are mutually attracted, but he tells her he can no longer see her when Li Po, a gunrunner, offers Jackson a job on a ship being used to deliver arms to Anti–Communist provinces. Wildeth stows away on the ship. When she is discovered, Jackson leaves her at a waterfront mission which is then attacked by the Communists. Jackson's ship engages the Communist forces in battle. When the enemy is defeated, he is reinstated in the Navy and marries Wildeth.

Comments: This drama with an unexpected political slant was one of the earliest Hollywood films to deal with Communist aggression in China, the action spiced with a romance between the Tracy and Wray characters. The two leads complimented each other nicely onscreen and, as Wray recalled in her autobiography *On the Other Hand*, Tracy paid her a compliment by asking her for an autographed photo after filming. *Shanghai Madness* was produced by Fox (not yet 20th Century–Fox) on a five-week schedule from June to July of '35. Wray was not the first choice for her role; Claire Trevor had originally been cast. MGM's Elizabeth Allan was considered next, before the producers settled on Wray.

One Sunday Afternoon

Paramount, 1933; *Released:* September 1, 1933; *Producer:* Louis D. Lighton, *Director:* Stephen Roberts, *Screenplay:* Grover Jones, William Slavens McNutt, Based on the play by James Hagan; *Photography:* Victor Milner, Karl Struss; *Camera Operators:* William Mellor, Clifford Blackstone, George Clemens; *Assistant Cameramen:* Guy Roe, E. F. Adams, Fleet Southcott; *Special Effects:* Gordon Jennings; *Process Photography:* Farciot Edouart; *Art Director:* Hans Dreier, W. B. Ihnen; *Film Editor:* Ellsworth Hoaglund; *Costumes:* Travis Banton; *Recording Engineers:* Harry D. Mills, Harold Lewis; *Chief Electricians:* Karl Gotham, Howard Kelly; *Chief Grip:* Wade Carley. Props: Lou Asher; *Still Photography:* William Walling, Jr., *Assistant Directors:* Jack Vorshell, Russell Matthews (85 minutes)

Songs: "Bill Bailey, Won't You Please Come Home," music and lyrics by Hughie Cannon, "In the Good Old Summertime," music by George Evans, lyrics by Ren Shields, "Good-bye, Little Girl, Good-bye," music by Gus Edwards, lyrics by Will D. Cobb, "Wait 'Til the Sun Shines," Nellie, music by Harry von Tilzer, lyrics by Andrew B. Sterling, "The Last Rose of Summer" and "Ach du Lieber Augustine," composer(s) unknown.

Cast: Gary Cooper (Lucius "Biff" Grimes), Fay Wray (Virginia Brush), Neil Hamilton (Hugo Barnstead), Roscoe Karns (Snappy Downer), Frances Fuller (Amy Lind), Jane Darwell (Mrs. Lind), Clara Blandick (Mrs. Brush), Sam Hardy

One Sunday Afternoon: With Gary Cooper

(Dr. Startzman), Harry Schults (Schneider), James Burtis (Dink Hoops), A. S. Byron (Foreman), Jack Clifford (Watchman), Carmencita Johnson, Johnny St. Claire

Synopsis: Small-town dentist Biff Grimes is obsessed with local beauty Virginia Brush (FW), ignoring Virginia's affection for his rival Hugo Barnstead, and remaining oblivious to Virginia's shy friend Amy, who loves Biff.

Rebuffed by Virginia, who elopes with Hugo, Biff eventually marries Amy, but continues to pine for Virginia. He eventually realizes his own stupidity when Virginia and Hugo return to town years later, and Virginia's crass appearance and flirtatious manner convince him that he married the right girl after all.

Comments: This gentle small-town comedy was well-directed by Stephen Roberts, with excellent performances from the entire cast. Wray, returning to Paramount for the first time since her studio contract had been terminated two years earlier, looked beautiful in her turn-of-the-century period costumes, and she was well-cast opposite her former Paramount co-star Gary Cooper.

James Hagan's play, bought by Paramount for $26,000, proved to be a durable property; Warner Bros. later purchased the rights and made two films based on the property, *The Strawberry Blonde*, (1941), starring James Cagney, Olivia de Havilland, Jack Carson and Rita Hayworth (in Fay Wray's role), and *One Sunday Afternoon*, a 1949 version starring Dennis Morgan and Janis Paige. Both films were directed by Raoul Walsh. The original Paramount film was later suppressed only to unexpectedly reappear decades later on cable television to the delight of film buffs (and Fay Wray), who found that it compared favorably with the Warner Bros. remakes.

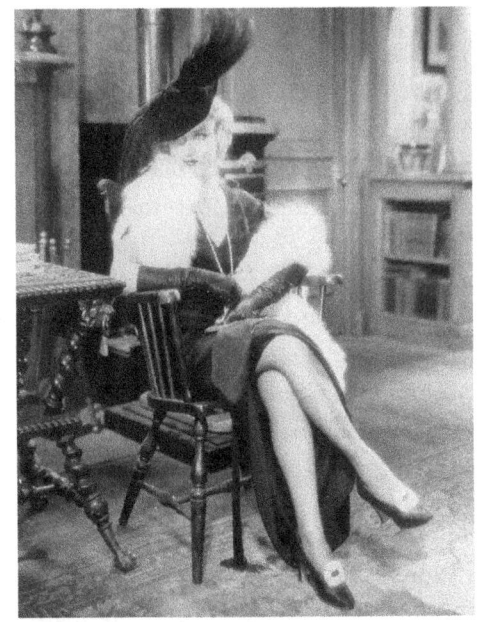

Top: One Sunday Afternoon; bottom: One Sunday Afternoon: With Frances Fuller (*right*) and Gary Cooper

Part II. Sound Films

The Bowery

20th Century-United Artists, 1933; *Released:* October 13, 1933; *Producers:* Darryl F. Zanuck, Joseph M. Schenck; *Associate Producers:* William Goetz, Raymond Griffith; *Director:* Raoul Walsh; *Screenplay:* Howard Estabrook, James Gleason, Based on the unpublished novel *Chuck Connors* by Michael L. Simmons, Bessie Roth Solomon; *Photography:* Barney McGill; *Camera Operators:* Bert Glennon, Stuart Thompson, Russell Metty; *Assistant Cameramen:* Harry Webb, Hal Carney; *Art Director:* Richard Day; *Film Editor:* Allen McNeill; *Cutter:* Ray Curtiss; *Wardrobe:* Peg O'Neill; *Music Director:* Alfred Newman; *Choreography:* Jack Haskell; *Sound Mixer:* Hugo Grenzbach; *Assistant Sound Engineers:* Jack Noyes, Don Oswald; *Production Manager:* Ed Ebele; *Chief Electrician:* Don Carstenson; *Chief Grip:* Tex Hayes; *Props:* L. Hafley; *Assistant Propman:* Don Greenwood; *Still Photography:* Kenneth Alexander; *Assistant Directors:* Fred Fox, Bill Forsyth (90 minutes)

Cast: Wallace Beery (Chuck Connors), George Raft (Steve Brody), Jackie Cooper (Swipes McGurk), Fay Wray (Lucy Calhoun), Pert Kelton (Trixie Odbray), Herman Bing (Max Herman), Oscar Apfel (Ivan Rummel), Ferdinand Munier (Honest Mike), George Walsh (John L. Sullivan), Lillian Harmer (Carrie A. Nation), Charles Lane (Doctor), Harold Huber (Slick), Fletcher Norton (Googy), Warren Hymer (Lumpy Hogan), Esther Muir (The Tart), John Bleifer (The Mute), Tammany Young (Chuck's Henchman), Frank Moran, Fred Behrle, Willie Keeler (Henchmen)

Synopsis: In New York's Bowery during the 1890s, volunteer firemen Chuck Connors and Steve Brody are friendly, boisterous rivals. Connors, who owns a saloon, gives shelter to Lucy Calhoun (FW), a young homeless girl who is invited to live in an upstairs apartment with Chuck's young pal Swipes McGurk.

The Bowery

Top: The Bowery: With Wallace Beery; *bottom: The Bowery*: With George Raft

Lucy falls in love with Chuck's rival Steve Brody, who tells her that he plans to open a saloon bigger than Chuck's. To gain brewery support for his venture, Steve tries to generate publicity by announcing that he will jump off the Brooklyn Bridge. He plans for Swipes to throw a dummy off the bridge in his place, but when the dummy is missing, Steve actually makes the jump himself before a crowd of thousands and is cheered as a hero afterwards. When Chuck decides to enlist and go to Spain in the war of 1898, Steve decides to join him despite their continuing rivalry, and Lucy kisses them both goodbye.

The Bowery

Comments: This period comedy-drama is not only well-done, it is an important film in Hollywood history since it was the first production of producer Darryl F. Zanuck's newly established 20th Century Pictures, which was soon to merge with Fox to become 20th Century–Fox. The unpublished novel that served as the basis for this film had been submitted to Zanuck the year before during his tenure at Warner Bros., but had not been produced by the studio. Based on historical figures (Raft's character, Steve Brody, had supposedly actually jumped off the Brooklyn Bridge and survived), the film was initially the focus of threatened lawsuits that were either dismissed or failed to materialize. Originally, Clark Gable (to have been loaned by MGM for the role of Brody) and Clara Bow (on the comeback trail after her career had collapsed in scandal) were slated to be cast. Director Raoul Walsh made no secret of the fact that he was frustrated during shooting by the antics of Beery and Raft, who were as combative off-screen as on; however, he had high praise for Wray's professionalism and her acting. As she had proven in *One Sunday Afternoon*, she was well-suited for period costume roles such as this. A popular film, *The Bowery* was re-released by 20th Century–Fox in 1948.

Master of Men

Columbia, 1933; *Released:* October 28, 1933; *Associate Producer:* Robert North; *Director:* Lambert Hillyer; *Screenplay:* Edward E. Paramore, Jr., Seton I. Miller; *Story:* Chester Erskin, Eugene Solow; *Photography:* Joseph August; *Film Editor:* Gene Havlick; *Sound Engineer:* Wilbur Brown; *Assistant Director:* Wilbur McGaugh (65 minutes)

Cast: Jack Holt (Buck Garrett), Fay Wray (Kay Walling), Theodore Von Eltz (Grenaker), Walter Connolly (Sam Parker), Berton Churchill (Mr. Walling)

Synopsis: Visiting her father's steel mill, Kay Walling is saved from injury in an industrial accident when crane operator Buck Garrett rescues her. Kay's powerful and ruthless father has Buck promoted to personnel manager after Buck organizes a workers' strike and impresses Walling with his leadership abilities.

Buck discovers that Walling and Grenaker, Walling's crooked associate, are trying to maneuver majority stockholder Sam Parker, Buck's friend, out of the business. Forewarned by Buck, Parker uses his business acumen to gain control of the mill and force Walling and Grenaker out instead.

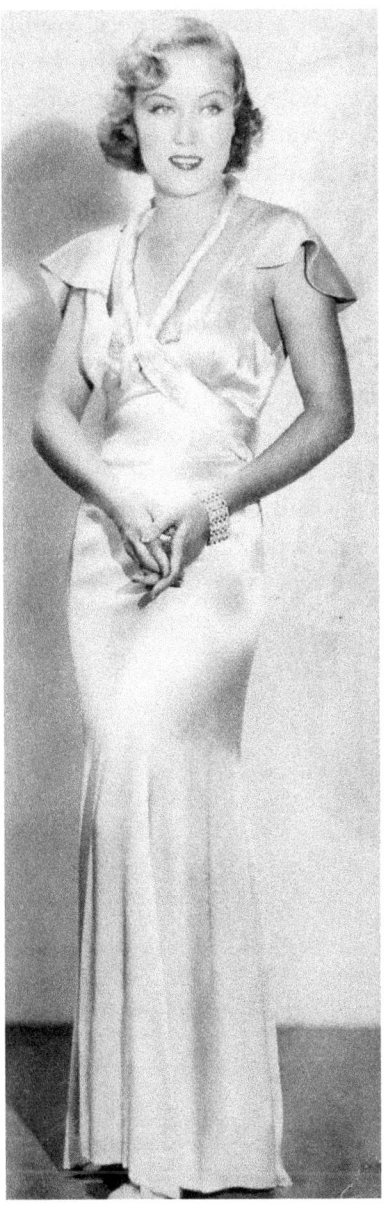

Master of Men

With his friend Parker now running the mill, Buck is appointed president, and marries Kay despite the objections of her father. Moving to New York with

Part II. Sound Films

Kay, he accumulates great wealth through various investments and, forgetting his working-class roots, closes the mill.

Buck goes bankrupt in the stock market crash of 1929 and very nearly loses Kay, who is alienated by his callousness. He finally succeeds in regaining Kay's love and the respect of the disenfranchised workers in his home town when he reopens the mill and stabilizes the local economy.

Comments: Columbia again paired Wray with Jack Holt in this minor drama. The plot seemed more suited to the Warner Bros. "social protest" films of the same period. Filmed on a four-week schedule during August and September of '33, the working title of this film was *Man of Steel.* Director Lambert Hillyer, an important name in the silent era, was on the downslide after the arrival of sound; nevertheless, he was a solid craftsman, and much more capable than most in Columbia's directorial stable. He would eventually direct one of the studio's better—and most underrated—Saturday matinee serials, *Batman* (1943), which marked the first screen appearance of the comic book character.

Madame Spy

Madame Spy: Universal Pictures portrait

Universal, 1934; *Released:* January 8, 1934; *Producer:* Carl Laemmle, Jr.; *Associate Producer:* Edmund Grainger; *Director:* Karl Freund; *Screenplay:* Johannes Brandt, Josef Than, Max Kimmich, From the novel *Unter falscher Flagge* by Max Kimmich; *Photography:* Edward Snyder, Norbert Brodine; *Art Director:* Charles D. Hall; *Supervising Film Editor:* Maurice Pivar; *Film Editor:* David Berg; *Music:* Giuseppe Becce, Heinz Roemheld, Pyotr Ilyich Tchaikovsky, Henryk Wieniawski, Franz Liszt, Jacques Offenbach, Johann Strauss; *Stock Music:* W. Franke Harling, David Klatzkin (70 minutes)

Cast: Fay Wray (Maria/B-

Madame Spy: With Edward Arnold

24), Nils Asther (Capt. Franck), Edward Arnold (Schultz), John Miljan (Capt. Weber), David Torrence (Seefeldt), Douglas Walton (Karl), Oscar Apfel (Pahlke), Vince Barnett (Peter), Robert Ellis (Sulkin), Alden [Stephen] Chase (Petroskie), Rollo Lloyd (Baum), Noah Beery (Gen. Philipow), A. S. Byron, Arthur Wanzer (Chemists), Ferdinand Schumann-Heink (Cafe Owner), Herbert Holcolmbe (Orderly), Reginald Pasch (Dumb Guy), Ruth Fallows (Lulu), Mabel Marden (Rosa), Robert Graves, Anders Van Haden (Detectives), Werner Plack (Conductor), Edward Peil, Sr. (Garage Proprietor), Albert J. Smith (Lackey), Philip Morris (Russian Officer), Eddy Chandler (Austrian Officer), Henry Grobel (Austrian Aviator), Jerry Jerome (Russian Aviator)

Synopsis: During World War I, German intelligence officer Capt. Franck falls in love with and marries a nurse named Maria (FW) who, unknown to him, is really a Russian spy known as B-24. Maria genuinely loves Franck, but when her brother Karl is murdered she realizes that her true identity is about to be revealed. She flees, returning to Russia.

Finally discovering Maria's secret, Franck, enraged by her duplicity, pursues

Madame Spy portrait

her, and Maria, wrongly blaming Franck for Karl's death, has him arrested in Russia. When she learns that another spy, Sulkin, was actually responsible for her brother's death, she helps Franck to escape.

Maria is convicted of treason and sentenced to death, but as she awaits execution a riot erupts in Warsaw. During the ensuing chaos, Franck, his faith in her restored, arrives and rescues her.

Comments: In a co-production deal with Germany's Tobis Films, Universal produced *Unter falscher Flagge* in Germany in 1932, with the understanding that Universal would reshoot the film in America with an American cast. The German version was directed by Johannes Meyer and starred Charlotte Susa and Gustav Frohlich (*Metropolis*). Reportedly, some long shots from the German original were re-used in the American remake.

Director Karl Freund, one of the greatest cinematographers in the history of film, had laid the groundwork for Universal's now-classic horror movies of the early 1930s, shooting *Dracula* and *Murders in the Rue Morgue* (both with Bela Lugosi) and directing *The Mummy* (with Boris Karloff). Freund helmed only a few movies before returning to cinematography for the remainder of his career.

Once to Every Woman

Columbia, 1934; *Released:* January 15, 1934; *Supervising Producer:* Robert North; *Director:* Lambert Hillyer; *Screenplay:* Jo Swerling, Based on the short story *Kaleidoscope in K* by A. J. Cronin; *Photography:* John Stumar; *Film Editor:* Richard Cahoon; *Sound Engineer:* Vernon Ashdown (70 minutes)

Cast: Ralph Bellamy (Dr. Jim Barclay), Fay Wray (Mary Fanshawe), Walter Connolly (Dr. Walter Selby), Mary Carlisle (Doris Andros), Walter Byron (Dr. Preston), J. Farrell MacDonald (Flannigan), Billie Seward (No. 5), Georgia Caine (Jeff), Katherine Clare Ward (Mrs. Flannigan), Mary Foy (Miss Baxter), Ben Alexander (Joe), Rebecca Wassem (Gail Drake), Leila Bennett (Sally), Jane Darwell (Mrs. Wood), Nora Cecil (Baxter's Sister), Edward LeSaint (Priest)

Synopsis: Dedicated nurse Mary Fanshawe (FW) falls in love with Dr. Preston, a philanderer. Blindly devoted to him, she resents Dr. Jim Barclay, an accomplished young surgeon in competition with Dr. Preston. When the hospital's chief surgeon, Dr. Selby, nearly botches an operation, it is then successfully completed by Dr. Barclay. Selby decides to retire, and appoints Barclay his successor.

Mary is disillusioned when she discovers that Dr. Preston has been cheating on her with Doris Andros, a junior nurse. She finds new hope when Dr. Barclay expresses interest in her, and begins to fall in love with him.

Comments: This convoluted *Dr. Kildare*–like hospital soap opera was Wray's second film with director Lambert Hillyer, and she was well-cast as a dedicated nurse who deals with the romantic entanglements of her own life as she attends to the physical and psychological needs of various patients. This was Wray's second

Part II. Sound Films

Once to Every Woman

movie with co-star Ralph Bellamy; they would become something of a lower-rung team, appearing in five movies together.

The Countess of Monte Cristo

Universal, 1934; *Released:* March 19, 1934; *Producer:* Stanley Bergerman; *Director:* Karl Freund; *Screenplay:* Karen DeWolf, Gene Lewis, Based on the German film *Die Graefin von Monte Cristo*, written by Walter Reisch, with contributions by Norman Krasna and Earl Snell; *Dialogue:* Gladys Unger; *Dialogue Director:* Gene Lewis; *Photography:* Charles Stumar, *Art Director:* Stanley Fleischer; *Film Editor:* Philip Kahn; *Supervising Film Editor:* Maurice Pivar, *Music Director:* Edward Ward; *Sound:* Gilbert Kurland; *Production Manager:* M. F. Murphy; *Assistant Directors:* Phil Karlstein [Karlson], Vic Noerdlinger; *Script Clerk:* Myrtle Gibson; *Supervising Secretary:* Peggy Vaughn, Song "No One Worries, No One Cares," composer unknown (78 minutes)

The Countess of Monte Cristo

Cast: Fay Wray (Janet Kruegar), Paul Lukas (Rumowski), Patsy Kelly (Mimi Schmidt), Reginald Owen (The Baron), Paul Page (Stefan), Robert McWade (Hotel Manager), Richard Tucker (Movie Director), John Sheehan (Sterner), Dewey Robinson (Proprietor of Exchange), Bobby Watson (Hotel Valet), Harvey Clarke (Newspaper Editor), Frank Reicher (Police Commissioner), Matthew Betz (Rumowski's Valet), Carmel Myers (Flower Girl), A. S. Byron (Stefan's Friend), Jack Cheatham (Doorman), Milton Owen (Desk Clerk), Alphonse Martell, George Hackathorne (Head Waiters)

Synopsis: Janet Kruegar (FW), an extra working at a movie studio in Vienna, is cast as a wealthy countess in a small role. When her performance is belittled by a director, she drives off the set and the lot with her friend Mimi, who had been cast as her maid.

Still in costume, they continue on in their roles, uncertain about what to do next, bluffing their way into a lavish hotel suite. Janet and Mimi become involved with a thief who discovers Janet's masquerade and forces her to continue, but she and Mimi are eventually arrested.

Janet calls her boyfriend Stefan, a newspaper reporter, for help, and Stefan publishes Janet's story. The movie studio offers Janet a contract as a result of the publicity, and she and Stefan marry.

Comments: The Countess of Monte Cristo, like *Madame Spy*, was an American remake of a recent German production, Ufa Studio's *Die Graefin von Monte Cristo*, released in 1932. The German original was directed by Karl Hartl and starred Brigitte Helm (the robot in *Metropolis*), in the role later played by Wray. Wray was well-cast and interacted well with comic foil Patsy Kelly, on loan from producer Hal Roach.

This was Wray's second film with director Karl Freund; although Freund had a reputation as being domineering and unpleasant, Wray had nothing but positive remarks to make about Freund when she discussed him with co-author Kinnard in 1993, praising his craftsmanship, skill and artistry.

The Countess of Monte Cristo, like *Madame Spy*, has not been distributed for years. The film was remade (reportedly using a few shots from the Freund version) by Universal-International in 1948, the new picture starring Sonja Henie and directed by Frederick de Cordova.

Black Moon

Columbia, 1934; *Released:* June 15, 1934; *Associate Producer:* Everett Riskin; *Director:* Roy William Neill; *Screenplay:* Wells Root, Based on the novel by Clements

Part II. Sound Films

Black Moon: With Jack Holt

Ripley; *Photography:* Joseph August; *Camera Operator:* Dave Ragin; *Assistant Cameramen:* Marcel Grand, Jack Andersen; *Film Editor:* Richard Cahoon; *Sound Engineer:* Edward Bernds; *Grip:* Eddie Blaisdell; *Props:* Stanley Dunn; *Choreography:* Max Scheck; *Technical Advisor:* Don Taylor; *Assistant Director:* Robert Margolis; *Still Photography:* Irving Lippman (68 minutes)

Cast: Jack Holt (Stephen Lane), Fay Wray (Gail), Dorothy Burgess (Juanita Lane), Cora Sue Collins (Nancy Lane), Arnold Korff (Dr. Perez), Clarence Muse (Lunch), Eleanor Wesselhoeft (Anna), Madame Sul-te-wan (Riva), Lawrence Criner (Kala), Lumsden Hare (Macklin), Henry Kolker (Doctor), Theresa Harris (Sacrificed Girl), Fred Walton (Butler), Billy McClain, Charles Moore, Robert Frazier, Ada Penn, Anna Lee Johnson (House Servants), Lillian West (Maid), Lillian Smith (Nurse), Grace Chapman (Welfare Worker), Edna Franklin (Girl Sacrificed by Mother), William H. Dunn (Langa)

Synopsis: Stephen Lane, troubled by his wife Juanita's unemotional distance from him and their daughter Nancy, sends her to a psychiatrist, who diagnoses Mrs. Lane as suffering from a neurosis. When Juanita tells Jim that she longs to return to her uncle's estate near Haiti where she spent her childhood, Stephen agrees, but only if she will allow her secretary Gail (FW) to go along for companionship and protection. Unknown to Stephen, though, Juanita had been inducted into a voodoo cult as a child, and is now being influenced by the cult from afar. When they arrive at the estate of Juanita's uncle, Juanita becomes more abusive toward Nancy; Gail, worried, sends for Stephen.

When Stephen arrives, he finds that Nancy's nurse has been killed and that Juanita's behavior has grown even more bizarre. Stephen follows Juanita one night as she wanders away to the beat of voodoo drums, and discovers that she is a high priestess in a voodoo cult about to sacrifice a young girl. To save the girl, Stephen shoots a voodoo priest, killing him.

After Juanita kidnaps her own daughter as a voodoo sacrifice, Stephen follows them and kills his now-possessed wife, escaping from the island with Gail and Nancy.

Comments: A voodoo thriller set in Haiti, *Black Moon* is not *quite* classifiable as a horror film, but it certainly merits at least cursory identification with the genre. Co-author Roy Kinnard interviewed three individuals connected with the production of this film: Fay Wray, sound engineer Edward Bernds and still photographer Irving Lippman; none had much to say about it, perhaps because it had been out of circulation and unseen for so long. Bernds drew a complete blank, Lippman remembered the picture only vaguely, and even Wray, usually reliable in accurately recalling her work, had little to say. "*Black Moon* is a film I've almost erased from my consciousness. I've *never* seen it, but I think it was supposed to be a pretty interesting story."

Director Roy William Neill was a reliable, underrated craftsman who certainly knew how to generate the sort of visual atmosphere a subject like this required. He would eventually direct most of Universal's Basil Rathbone *Sher-*

lock Holmes thrillers, *Frankenstein Meets the Wolf Man* and the Boris Karloff melodrama *The Black Room*. Ed Bernds *did* recall Neill from his work on other Columbia films, remembering him as an unassuming director of high quality and an expert in camera placement who could obtain a great deal of impact from his limited B-picture budgets. *Black Moon* finally *was* exhumed from Columbia's vaults after decades, turning up on cable television. The film's atmospherics offer further proof of Neill's considerable talent.

Viva Villa!

Metro-Goldwyn-Mayer, 1934; *Released:* April 27, 1934; *Producer:* David O. Selznick; *Director:* Jack Conway; *Additional Direction (uncredited):* Howard Hawks, William Wellman; *Screenplay:* Ben Hecht, Suggested by the book *Pancho Villa* by Edgcumb Pinchon, O. B. Stade, with contributions from James K. McGuiness, Howard Emmett Rogers; *Photography:* James Wong Howe, Charles

Viva Villa! original release lobby card

G. Clarke; *Additional Photography:* Clyde De Vinna; *Transitional Visual Effects:* Slavko Vorkapich; *Art Director:* Harry Oliver; *Film Editor:* Robert J. Kern; *Interior Decorator:* Edwin B. Willis; *Wardrobe:* Dolly Tree; *Music Score:* Herbert Stothart; *Music Consultant:* Juan Aguilar; *Orchestrators:* Charles Maxwell, Paul Marquardt, Maurice de Packh, Wayne Allen, David Snell; *Recording Director:* Douglas Shearer; *Sound Recordist:* Mike McLaughlin; *Sound Mixers:* Stan Lambert, James Brock; *Assistant Directors:* John Waters, Red Golden, Arthur Rosson; *Second Unit Directors:* Arthur Rosson, Dick

*Top: **Viva Villa!**:* MGM studio portrait; *bottom: **Viva Villa!**:* With Wallace Beery (*right*)

Rosson; *Technical Advisor:* Carlos Navarro; *Technical Associate:* Matias Santoyo; *General Press Agent:* Howard Dietz (112 minutes)

Cast: Wallace Beery (Pancho Villa), Leo Carrillo (Sierra), Fay Wray (Teresa), Donald Cook (Don Felipe), Stuart Erwin (Johnny Sykes), Henry B. Walthall (Francisco Madero), Joseph Schildkraut (Gen. Pascal), Katherine de Mille (Rosita), George E. Stone (Emilio Chavita), Phillip Cooper (Pancho, the Boy), David Durand (Bugler Boy), Frank Puglia (Villa's Father), Francis X. Bushman (Calloway), Adrian Rosley (Mendoza Brother), Henry Armetta (Mendoza Brother), Pedro Regas (Member of Pascal's Staff), George Regas (Don Rodrigo), John Merkyl (Pascal's Aide), Charles Stewart (Member of Pascal's Staff), Steve Clemento (Member of Pascal's Staff), Carlos De Valdez (Old Man), Harry Cording (Majordomo), Sam Godfrey (Prosecuting Attorney), Nigel De Brulier (Political Judge), Charles Requa, Tom Ricketts (Grandees), Clarence Hummel Wilson (Jail Official), James Martin (Mexican Officer), Anita Gordiana (Dancer), Francis McDonald (Villa's Man), Harry Semels (Soldier), Julian Rivero (Telegraph Operator), Bob McKenzie (Bartender), Dan Dix (Drunkard), Paul Stanton (Newspaper Man), Mischa Auer (Military Attaché), Belle Mitchell (Spanish Wife), John Davidson, Brandon Hurst, Leonard Mudie (Statesmen), Herbert Prior, Emile Chautard (Generals), Hector Sarno (Mendoza Brother), Ralph Bushman (Calloway), Arthur Treacher (English Reporter), William von Brincken (German Reporter), Andre Cheron (French Reporter), Michael Visaroff (Russian Reporter), Shirley Chambers (Wrong Girl), Arthur Thalasso (Butcher), Chris Pin Martin, Nick De Ruiz (Peons)

Synopsis: In the 1880s, Mexican bandit Pancho Villa has gained a reputation as a champion of the poor as he steals from the wealthy and opposes those who would exploit his countrymen. His legend grows when Johnny Sykes, an American reporter, befriends Villa and writes flattering stories publicizing his exploits.

Villa eventually forms and leads a revolutionary army against the dictatorial reign of President Porfirio Diaz, who soon abdicates and is succeeded by Villa's ally Francisco Madero. At Madero's urging, Villa disbands his army. When Madero is assassinated by Gen. Pascal, Villa regroups his forces to oust the usurper.

Longing to possess Teresa (FW), the beautiful sister of aristocratic revolutionary Don Felipe, Villa is enraged when she rejects him. He tries to rape her, and as they struggle, Villa's bloodthirsty henchman Sierra shoots and kills her. Pascal is overthrown and killed. When Villa is installed as the new leader of Mexico, he is overwhelmed by the problems of running the country and eventually gives up his authority.

Returning to his hometown of Chihuahua, Villa is assassinated by a crazed Don Felipe as he talks with Johnny Sykes.

Comments: MGM's biopic about famed Mexican revolutionary Pancho Villa ("fiction woven from truth," as an opening title informs the audience) was one of the biggest films produced in Hollywood before producer David O. Selznick's *Gone with the Wind*. Like *Gone with the Wind*, it was a troubled undertaking from the start. After filming began on location in Mexico with Howard Hawks directing second-unit material, actor Lee Tracy (Wray's co-star in *Doctor X*), originally cast in the role of reporter Johnny Sykes, nearly provoked an international incident due to an insult (the exact nature of which varies from account to account) that he allegedly made to Mexican soldiers during filming. An apologetic Tracy later claimed that the facts had been distorted and blown out of proportion, but nevertheless, he was promptly fired and his studio contract was cancelled by MGM.

Mexican officials also objected to the casting of Beery (known primarily for comedic roles) as Villa, and to MGM's general approach to the subject. Additionally, some second-unit footage shot by Hawks was destroyed when the airplane flying back to the U.S. crashed. Despite these setbacks, and continuing friction between the two governments over the Tracy affair and other matters, second-unit shooting was completed in Mexico by mid–December 1933. Over 70 reels of battle footage were produced, after which the company returned to shoot the remainder of the film in and around Hollywood.

By this point, Howard Hawks had been replaced as director by MGM's top action specialist Jack Conway, and most of the principal cast had been replaced, including Mona Maris as Teresa. Several actresses were tested as replacements for Maris, including Myrna Loy, Carmel Myers, Lila Lee and Dorothy Burgess before Selznick settled on Fay Wray. This was Wray's first and only starring role for MGM (she *was* cast in that studio's *Society Doctor* the next year, but cancelled before filming), and she acquits herself well in her ethnic characterization. She wisely attempts no accent here, as she did with disastrous results in *Captain Thunder*, instead relying on the elaborate make-up and costuming to provide flavor. The trade paper *Variety*, in its review of the film on April 17, 1934, commented: "The two principal (female roles) are well-handled by Fay Wray as the sympathetic aristocrat who is brutally assaulted and assassinated by Villa, and Katherine de Mille (Cecil's daughter, who manifests much talent) likewise stands out."

Viva Villa! was a major hit on release, with tickets for the New York showing costing $2.20. The *Film Daily* critics selecting it as one of the ten best of 1934.

Part II. Sound Films

The Affairs of Cellini

20th Century-United Artists, 1934; *Released:* August 24, 1934; *Producers:* Darryl F. Zanuck, Joseph M. Schenck; *Associate Producers:* William Goetz, Raymond Griffith; *Director:* Gregory La Cava; *Screenplay:* Bess Meredyth; Adaptation by Fred de Gresac, Based on the play *The Firebrand* by Edwin Justus Mayer; *Pho-*

The Affairs of Cellini portrait

Top: The Affairs of Cellini: With Frank Morgan; *bottom: The Affairs of Cellini*: With Fredric March

Part II. Sound Films

The Affairs of Cellini: With Fredric March

tography: Charles Rosher; *Camera Operators:* Roy Tripp, Roy Clark; *Assistant Cameramen:* William Reinhold; *Art Director:* Richard Day; *Film Editor:* Barbara McLean; *Sound:* Thomas T. Moulton; *Costume Design:* Gwen Wakeling; *Costumes:* United Costumers, Inc.; *Music Score:* Alfred Newman; *Ballet Master:* Adolph Bolm; *Assistant Director:* Fred Fox; *Still Photographer:* Clarence Hewitt (80 minutes)

Cast: Constance Bennett (Duchess of Florence), Fredric March (Benvenuto Cellini), Frank Morgan (Alessandro, Duke of Florence), Fay Wray (Angela), Vince Barnett (Ascanio), Jessie Ralph (Beatrice), Louis Calhern (Ottaviano), Jay Eaton (Polverino), Paul Harvey (Emissary), John Rutherford (Captain of Guards), Irene Ware (Daughter of the Royal House of Bocci), Ward Bond (Palace Guard), Dewey Robinson (Steward), Constantine Romanoff (Man in Dungeon), Lucille Ball (Lady in Waiting), Lionel Belmore (Court Member), Lane Chandler (Jailer), James Flavin (Guard), Theodore Lorch (Executioner), Russ Powell (Servant), Harry Wilson (Henchman)

Synopsis: Benvenuto Cellini, a sixteenth-century Italian rogue, has earned a mixed reputation with Florentine royalty through his abilities as a goldsmith, a sculptor and a lover. Cellini is sentenced to hang for one of his many transgressions, but he avoids the noose by assigning his beautiful model Angela (FW) to the court of Duke Allesandro.

While the Duke is preoccupied in his attempts to seduce Angela, Cellini becomes intimate with the Duke's wife. The Duke learns of this and again orders Cellini's death. The Duke later agrees to free Cellini when he is promised that Angela will be at his upcoming banquet.

When the Duchess sees Angela at the Banquet, the Duke lies and tells his wife that Angela is engaged to Cellini. Jealous, the Duchess gives Cellini poisoned wine, commanding him to toast his bride. When Cellini, pretending to die from the poison, falls to the floor, the Duchess expresses her love for him, angering the Duke. The Duchess then tells the Duke that she is taking Cellini with her to another palace. The Duke objects at first, but calms down when he realizes that Angela can then stay with him.

Comments: Shot in four weeks during February and March of '34, Fox's *The Affairs of Cellini* initially ran into trouble with the draconian Hays censorship office due to the producers failing to obtain prior clearance on the material, despite assurances from producer Zanuck that the script would be sanitized, with references to the various characters' sexual promiscuity eliminated. Zanuck originally had intended to cast Charles Laughton in Frank Morgan's role, but Laughton was then under contract to Paramount and Zanuck was unable to reach an agreement with the studio. Once again Wray looked beautiful in period costumes, but was somewhat miscast as Cellini's dimwitted model Angela, a flighty character seemingly better-suited to Gracie Allen.

The Richest Girl in the World

RKO-Radio, 1934; *Released:* September 21, 1934; *Producer:* Pandro S. Berman; *Director:* William A. Seiter; *Story and Screenplay:* Norman Krasna, with contributions by Leona D'Ambry, Glenn Tryon, Jerry Hutchinson; *Continuity:* Leona D'Ambry; *Photography:* Nicholas Musuraca; *Art Directors:* Van Nest Polglase, Charles Kirk; *Film Editor:* George Crone; *Music:* Max Steiner; *Sound:* John E. Tribby; *Assistant Director:* Rex Bailey (78 minutes)

Cast: Miriam Hopkins (Dorothy Hunter), Joel McCrea (Tony Travers), Fay Wray (Sylvia Lockwood), Henry Stephenson (John Connors), Reginald Denny (Phillip Lockwood), Beryl Mercer (Marie), George Meeker (Donald), Wade

Part II. Sound Films

The Richest Girl in the World fan magazine fashion promotion

Boteler (Jim Franey), Herbert Bunston (Cavendish), Burr McIntosh (David Preston), Edgar Norton (Binkley, the Butler), Fred Howard (Haley)

Synopsis: Sylvia Lockwood (FW), secretary to reclusive heiress Dorothy Hunter, has agreed to impersonate her wealthy boss at personal appearances so that Dorothy can avoid unwanted publicity, while Dorothy pretends to be Sylvia.

Donald, her fiancé, breaks off their engagement, and Dorothy is saddened when he remarks that, because of her wealth, no man could ever love her for herself. Having switched roles again, Dorothy, pretending to be Sylvia the secretary, meets and is infatuated with Tony Travers, playing a game of pool with him. Then she is angered when he takes Sylvia on a canoe ride, believing her to be Dorothy. She follows them in a motorboat, capsizing their canoe.

Luring Tony to a mountain retreat, Dorothy gradually falls in love with him, but is hurt when she realizes that she is a "consolation prize," since Tony thinks that Sylvia (posing as wealthy Dorothy) wouldn't accept him. When she finally is convinced of his love, though, Dorothy finally does marry Tony, continuing her impersonation during their honeymoon on a luxury liner.

Comments: Miriam Hopkins was borrowed from Paramount and Fay Wray from 20th Century Pictures (where she was briefly under contract) to star in this romantic comedy dealing with impersonation and mistaken identity. RKO paid young writer Norman Krasna $4,000 for his story, outbidding MGM for the property, with the original intention of using the material as a vehicle for Ann Harding.

The film's high quality is due to Krasna's script; he was nominated for an Academy Award in the Best Story category, losing to Arthur Caesar for MGM's Clark Gable–Spencer Tracy vehicle *Manhattan Melodrama*. *The Richest Girl In the World* was shot on a four-week schedule during July–August 1934, with some of the exteriors shot at Lake Arrowhead, California.

Cheating Cheaters

Universal, 1934; *Released:* November 5, 1934; *Executive Producer:* Carl Laemmle; *Producer:* Stanley Bergerman; *Director:* Richard Thorpe; *Screenplay:* Gladys Unger, Allen Rivkin, Based on the play by Max Marcin; *Additional Dialogue:* James Mulhauser; *Photography:* George Robinson; *Camera Operator:* Norbert Brodine; *Art Director:* Harrison Wiley; *Film Editor:* Ray Curtiss; *Supervising Film Editor:* Maurice Pivar; *Music Score:* Edward Ward, *Sound Engineer:* Gilbert Kurland; *Costumes:* Vera West; *Hairstyles:* Margaret Donovan; *Assistant Directors:* Phil Karlstein

[Karlson], Harry Mancke; *Script Clerk:* Jean Raymond; *Production Secretary:* Billy Moritz; Song "I've Burned My Bridges," music and lyrics by Barry Trivers, Arthur Morton (67 minutes)

Cast: Fay Wray (Nan Brockton), Cesar Romero (Tom Palmer), Minna Gombell (Nell Brockton), Henry Armetta (Prof. Toni Verdi), Francis L. Sullivan (Dr. George Brockton), Hugh O'Connell (Steve Wilson), Wallis Clark (Mr. Palmer), Ann Shoemaker (Mrs. Grace Palmer), John T. Murray (Ira Lazarre), George Berraud (Phil), Morgan Wallace (Holmes), Harold Huber (Edgar "Legs" Finelli), Reginald Barlow (Police Captain), Pat Flaherty (Gym Instructor), John Ince (Ship's Officer), Harry C. Bradley (Hanley), Lee Shumway, Edward Peil, Sr. (Detectives), Walter Brennan (Ship's Steward), King Baggott, Ed Haskett, Jr. (Officials), Billy West, Don Brodie (Clerks)

Synopsis: Nan Brockton (FW) and her father, Dr. George Brockton, are jewel thieves. When Tom Palmer meets them aboard an ocean liner returning from Europe, he is unaware of their criminal nature and, learning that they are living at a Long Island estate near his, invites them to a party at his home. (Tom Palmer and his family are also thieves, planning to rob the Brocktons.)

Nan successfully robs the Palmers' estate, stealing some jewels, but Tom and his "father" are caught by Nan's accomplices in their attempt to rob the Brocktons. The police surround and arrest all of them, but Tom is *Released:* into the custody of Nan, who is revealed to be an undercover police operative. She tells Tom that she is in love with him, and will be waiting for him when he is *Released:* from prison.

Comments: This heist comedy from Universal paired Wray with Cesar Romero. This potentially interesting film, with a good cast and solid production credits, has remained unseen for decades. Filmed in a brief two weeks during September of '34, this was the third film version of Max Marcin's 1916 play. The first had been filmed by C. K. Y. Film Corporation in 1919. Clara Kimball Young and Jack Holt starred, and the director was Allan Dwan. The second version, also filmed by C. K. Y., starred Betty Compson and Kenneth Harlan and was directed by Edward Laemmle in 1927.

Woman in the Dark

RKO-Radio, 1934; *Released:* November 9, 1934; *Associate Producer:* Burt Kelly; *Director:* Phil Rosen; *Screenplay:* Sada Cowan, Based on the short story *Woman In the Dark* by Dashiell Hammett; *Additional Dialogue:* Charles Williams, Marcy

Part II. Sound Films

Woman in the Dark

Klauber; *Photography:* Joseph Ruttenberg, Sam Leavitt; *Sets:* William Saulter; *Film Editor:* William Thompson; *Sound Engineer:* Dan Bloomberg; *Production Managers:* Phil Brandon, Ed Lavenstein; *Assistant Director:* Chris Butte (68 minutes)

Cast: Fay Wray (Louise Loring), Ralph Bellamy (John Bradley), Melvyn Douglas (Tony Robson), Roscoe Ates (Tommy Logan), Ruth Gillette (Lil Logan), Joe King (Detective), Nell O'Day (Helen Grant), Frank Otte (Kraus), Reed Brown, Jr. (Dick Conroy), Granville Bates (Sheriff Fred Grant), Charles Williams (Hotel Clerk), Frank Shannon, Clifford Dunston

Synopsis: Moving into his late father's house after serving time in prison for accidentally killing a man in a fight, John Bradley is visited by Helen Grant, the young woman he and the dead man had fought over. Helen has further romantic designs on John, but her plans are interrupted by the arrival of Louise Loring (FW).

Louise is trying to break away from her relationship with gangster Tony

Robson. Robson and his henchman Conroy pursue Louise to Bradley's house. Bradley stands up to them, defending Louise. After a fight, he forces them to leave, and Louise tells Bradley how her life has been dominated and controlled by Robson.

Conroy's skull had been fractured in the fight with Bradley, and Robson files a complaint against Bradley. Bradley learns of this and leaves town with Louise before the sheriff can arrest him. Bradley and Louise travel to the city, where they hide out with Tommy Logan, a prison friend of Bradley's. While staying there, they realize they love each other. Louise and Bradley are tracked to Logan's by the police. Bradley is shot as he tries to escape and Louise is arrested on charges that she stole jewelry from Robson. Bailed out of jail, Louise is told that Bradley is recovering in a hospital, and she decides to return to Robson. Eventually it is revealed that it was Robson, not Bradley, who delivered the blow to Conroy's head in the fight. Robson is arrested, and Bradley is cleared and reunites with Louise.

Comments: A crime melodrama with a better-than-average script, based on a Dashiell Hammett original. Hammett's name was "box office," especially after the release of MGM's *The Thin Man*, and even though Hammett did not contribute to the script, his name was featured above the main title in *Woman in the Dark*. The film was shot in three weeks during June and July of '34 at the Biograph Studios in New York.

White Lies

Columbia, 1934; *Released:* November 27, 1934; *Director:* Leo Bulgakov; *Story and Screenplay:* Harold Shumate; *Photography:* Benjamin Kline; *Film Editor:* Otto Meyer; *Sound Engineer:* Edward L. Bernds; *Assistant Director:* Edward Bernoudy (63 minutes)

Cast: Walter Connolly (John Frank Mitchell), Fay Wray (Joan Mitchell), Victor Jory (Terry Condon), Irene Hervey (Mary Mallory), Leslie Fenton (Dan Oliver), Robert Allen (Arthur Bradford), William Demarest (Al Roberts), Oscar Apfel (Hunter), Mary Foy (Mrs. Kelly), Katherine Clare Ward (Mrs. Egglesby), Harry C. Bradley (Davis), Robert E. O'Connor (Capt. McHenry), Charles C. Wilson (Defense Attorney), Wallis Clark (Prosecuting Attorney), Emmett Vogan (First Courtroom Prosecutor), Roger Grey (Manager of Employment Agency), Jessie Arnold (Mary's Landlady), Raymond Brown (Manager of Acme Paint Company), Lowden Adams (Butler), Bill James (Groom), Carlton E. Griffin (Clerk), Frank O'Connor (Sheriff), Bruce Mitchell (Baliff), Allyn Drake (Nurse), Dorothy

Part II. Sound Films

Shearer (Police Matron), Joe Heon (Newsboy), Harry Hume (Jury Foreman), Bud Geary (Chauffeur), Edith Craig (Miss Benson), Reginald Barlow, Edward LeSaint (Judges), Margaret Meighan

Synopsis: Newspaper editor John Frank Mitchell, pulled over in his car by traffic cop Terry Condon, defiantly tears up the ticket issued by Condon. Condon arrests him. At the police station, Mitchell's daughter Joan (FW) soothes her father's temper, and he pays the ticket. Condon is promoted to sergeant.

When Dan Oliver, an embezzler, threatens to kill Mitchell over an

White Lies: Columbia Pictures studio portrait; *bottom*: *White Lies*

Part II. Sound Films

White Lies

expose Mitchell intends to publish, Condon is assigned to investigate. Invited to dinner at Mitchell's home, Terry is attracted to Joan — and vice versa.

Oliver is arrested and tried, but at his trial he escapes, shooting Conroy with his own gun. When Joan, out of sympathy, tries to help Oliver's dejected fiancée Mary get her life in order, Oliver, still at large, kills Joan's former boyfriend Arthur Bradford and frames Joan for the murder.

Condon, recovered from the gunshot wound, is determined to free Joan. Mary knows the truth and testifies on Joan's behalf, and Joan is freed. Oliver tries to kill Mary, but Condon tracks him down and arrests him, handing Mitchell's paper a major scoop in the process.

Comments: This drama was made by Columbia to fulfill a pledge made by the Hollywood film industry to the Crime Commission in Washington D. C. The studios, in response to criticism, had agreed to take a more positive stance toward the nation's police officers and portray them with dignity on-screen. *White Lies* was the first of two Columbia films pairing Wray with Victor Jory.

Part II. Sound Films

Mills of the Gods

Columbia, 1934; *Released:* December 15, 1934; *Supervising Producer:* Robert North, *Director:* Roy William Neill, *Screenplay:* Garrett Fort, Based on the story *A Hundred Million Dollars* by Melville Baker, Jack Kirkland, Photography: Allen Siegler, Film Editor: Jack Rawlins, Sound Engineer: Edward L. Bernds, Assistant *Director:* Art Black (66 minutes)

Cast: May Robson (Mary Hastings), Fay Wray (Jean Hastings), Victor Jory (Jim Devlin), Raymond Walburn (Willard Hastings), James Blakely (Alex Hastings), Josephine Whittell (Henrietta Hastings), Mayo Methot (Sarah), Albert Conti (Count Filippo Di Fraschiani), Samuel S. Hinds (Burroughs), Willard Robertson (Thomas), Edward Keane (Morgan), Edward Van Sloan (Komeoski), Frank Reicher (Barrett), Fredrik Vogeding (Njordstron), Guy Usher (Kennedy), Eric Wilton (Thomas), Winter Hall (Bevins), Eddie Baker (Motorcycle Sergeant), George C. Pearce (Doctor), A. R. Haysel (Yard Master), Albert J. Smith (Switch-

Mills of the Gods

man), Sidney Bracy, James Millican (Chauffeurs), Burr Caruth (Gateman), Roger Gray (Chris), Charles McAvoy (Detective), Raymond Turner (Porter), Jack Richardson (Workman), Charles Marsh (Clerk), Earl Bunn (Machine Gunman), Dutch Hendrian (Brakeman), Bruce Mitchell, Frank Meredith, Arthur Thalasso, Frank G. Fanning (Guards), Jerry Storm (Waiter), Adda Gleason, Jack Mack, Freddie Gilman, Stanley G. Blystone, Edward Brady, May Foster, Joe Smith Marba, Hal Price, George Magrill, Gene Gehrung, Allan Sears, Joseph Henderson, Jack Lowe, Harry Semels, Frank O'Connor, Harry Wilson, James Mason, Edward Randall, Otto Gervice, Helen Geraghty, Robert Wiber, Stella LeSaint, Kathryn Winner, George Burton, Ralph Banks, Harry Hume, Tom London, Art Miles, Charles Speas, Rodney Hildebrand, Charles Hickman, Roy Borderoth, Fred Trowbridge, Mac Wright, Clarence L. Sherwood

Synopsis: Matriarch Mary Hastings, who has built her family business into a bustling industrial plant, is now approaching retirement. Refusing to entrust the business to her own family, she passes control to a board of directors made up of plant employees.

After her retirement, Mary realizes that she must act when the plant is nearly ruined in the Great Depression. She turns to her son Willard and daughter Henrietta for help. Willard recommends selling the plant, but is opposed by plant labor organizer Jim Devlin, who is in love with Mary's granddaughter Jean (FW).

A riot breaks out in town over the economic troubles at the plant, and Willard's son Alex is accidentally killed. Mary is able to raise badly needed cash and manages to reopen the plant, stabilizing the local economy as Jim and Jean continue their romance.

Comments: This social drama, dealing with the effects of the Great Depression on a small-town family-owned manufacturing plant, was Wray's second Columbia film with Victor Jory. Shot in three weeks in October–November of '34, it benefited from good direction by Roy William Neill and solid writing by Garrett Fort. According to sound engineer Edward L. Bernds, *Mills of the Gods* was jokingly retitled *Oh, God! The Mills Brothers!* on the set, referring to a popular singing group of the time.

Come Out of the Pantry

United Artists, 1935; *Released:* July 1935; *Producer:* Herbert Wilcox; *Director:* Jack Raymond; *Screenplay:* Austin Parker, Douglas Furber, A. E. Thomas, Based

Part II. Sound Films

on the play by Alice Duer Miller; *Photography:* Freddie Young; *Song:* "Everything Stops for Tea" by Al Goodhart, Al Hoffman, Maurice Sigler (73 minutes)

Cast: Jack Buchanan (Lord Robert Brent), Fay Wray (Hilda Beach-Howard), James Carew (Mr. Beach-Howard), Olive Blakeney (Mrs. Beach-Howard), Fred Emney (Lord Axminster), Kate Cutler (Lady Axminster), Ronald Squire (Eccles), Marie O'Neill (Mrs. Gore), Ethel Stewart (Rosie), Ben Welden (Tramp), W. T. Ellwanger (Porteous)

Synopsis: When Lord Herbert Brent finds that all of his money is gone, he is forced to work as a footman for Mr. and Mrs. Beach-Howard, New York millionaires. He then meets and falls in love with their niece Hilda (FW).

Comments: Come Out of the Pantry was the first of a quartet of films that Wray made in England, two of them with popular British star Jack Buchanan. At the time, the British film industry was making a concerted effort to gain wider distribution for their movies in America, and so imported American stars to increase the international appeal of their films. Although she enjoyed working with Buchanan, Wray told co-author Kinnard that she was less than impressed with the technical capability of the British film industry at that time and that, although she was treated with courtesy and professional respect, she did not feel that she was entirely welcome, sensing a degree of resentment

Come Out of the Pantry promotional cigarette card

Part II. Sound Films

A Gaumont-British promotional ad for American stars in British films

over the importation of American personalities. She reported that she *did* appreciate the no-nonsense contract she signed, which, unlike the usual convoluted agreements with Hollywood studios, was only two paragraphs long and completely free of confusing legalese!

The Clairvoyant

Gaumont-British, 1935; *Released:* July 15, 1935; *Producer:* Michael Balcon; *Director:* Maurice Elvey; *Screenplay:* Bryan Wallace, Robert Edmunds, Based on the novel by Ernst Lothar, English-language translation: B. Ryan; *Screen Adaptation:* Charles Bennett; *Photography:* Errol Hinds, Glen MacWilliams; *Film Editor:* Paul Capon; *Designers:* Joe Strassner, Alfred Junge; *Original Music:* Arthur Benjamin; *Music Director:* Louis Levy; *Costume Design:* Marianne, Joe Strassner; *Sound Engineer:* Harry Hand (72 minutes)

    Cast: Claude Rains (Maximus), Fay Wray (Renee Maximus), Jane Baxter (Christine), Ben Field (Simon), Mary Clare (Madame), Jack Raine (Customs

The Clairvoyant: With Claude Rains

Officer), Margaret Davidge (Lodging Housekeeper), C. Denier Warren (Bimeter), Donald Calthrop (Derelict), Graham Moffat (Page Boy), D. J. Williams (Juror)

Synopsis: Maximus, a mind-reader, gains notoriety when he foresees a train accident and saves the passengers, including his wife Renee (FW), by evacuating the train. Continuing with his act on the English music hall circuit, he accurately predicts horse race winners and a mine disaster. Maximus' abilities are genuine, but he realizes that he is only able to function as a clairvoyant while in the presence of Christine, daughter of a newspaper publisher. Maximus' dependency on Christine nearly ruins his marriage to Renee, but he and Renee reconcile after they overcome their difficulties.

Comments: "*The Clairvoyant* was ... a very interesting story," said Wray. "Claude Rains was a fine actor. It wasn't just a 'strange' movie, but had a lot of character development. Claude Rains played a fake mind-reader who began to believe in himself and make predictions that came true. He performed that so well."

Wray certainly holds her own opposite Rains, one of the screen's greatest actors. *The Clairvoyant* is borderline horror-fantasy, with the lighting on Rains' eyes during his mind-reading scenes recalling similar effects in *Dracula* and *Svengali*. *The Clairvoyant* was later abridged by a few minutes and retitled *The Evil Mind* in America. It is commonly available on home video under that title.

Bulldog Jack

Gaumont-British, 1935; *Released:* April 1935; *Producer:* Michael Balcon; *Director:* Walter Forde; *Screenplay:* Jack Hulbert; Based on characters created by H. C. "Sapper" McNeile; *Screen Adaptation:* J. O. C. Orton, Sidney Gilliat, Gerald Fairlie; *Photography:* Mutz Greenbaum; *Film Edi-

Bulldog Jack portrait

tor: Otto Ludwig; *Designer:* Alfred Junge; *Music Director:* Louis Levy; *Costumes:* Marianne, Joe Strassner; *Sound Engineer:* A. C. O'Donoghue (70 minutes)

Cast: Fay Wray (Ann Manders), Jack Hulbert (Jack Pennington, a.k.a. "Bulldog Drummond"), Claude Hulbert (Algy Longworth), Ralph Richardson (Morelle), Paul Graetz (Salvini), Gibb McLaughlin (Denny), Atholl Fleming (Bulldog Drummond), Henry Longhurst (McIvor), Cyril Smith (Duke)

Synopsis: Lovely Ann Manders (FW) is kidnapped by a gang of jewel thieves. Jack Pennington impersonates the famous sleuth Bulldog Drummond, who has been injured, and with his sidekick Algy Longworth trails the gang to their underground lair, saving Ann, who is held captive in a subway train.

Comments: The popular Bulldog Dummond detective character provided the basis for this semi-spoof. It was marketed as a more-or-less straight Drummond adventure in America, with the title changed to *Alias Bulldog Drummond* and much of the physical comedy eliminated, reducing the film's running time to 62 minutes.

When Knights Were Bold

CAP/FA, 1936; *Released:* February 19, 1936; *Producer:* Max Schach, C. M. Woolf; *Director:* Jack Raymond; *Screenplay:* Austin Parker, Douglas Furber, Based on a play by Harriett Jay [writing as Charles Marlowe]; *Photography:* Freddie Young; *Film Editor:* Frederick Wilson; *Art Director:* Wilfred Arnold; *Music:* Al Goodhart, Al Hoffman, Maurice Sigler; *Music Director:* Harry Perritt (76 minutes)

Cast: Jack Buchanan (Sir Guy de Vere), Fay Wray (Lady Rowena), Garry Marsh (Brian Ballymote), Kate Cutler (Aunt Agatha), Martita Hunt (Aunt Esther), Robert Horton (Cousin Bertie), Aubrey Mather (The Canon), Aubrey Fitzgerald (Barker), Robert Nainby (Whittle), Moore Marriott (The Tramp), Charles Paton (The Mayor)

Synopsis: After inheriting his ancestral estate, a British soldier clashes with his snobbish relatives. When he is accidentally knocked unconscious, he experiences a medieval fantasy in which he romances Lady Rowena (FW).

Comments: This comedic fantasy was Wray's fourth and last British movie. American distributors were reluctant to pick up this film, perhaps out of fear that its British subject would not play well across the Atlantic; it was not shown in the U.S. until 1942, six years later, and for that release was severely trimmed to a running time of only 57 minutes.

Part II. Sound Films

When Knights Were Bold: With Jack Buchanan

Roaming Lady

Columbia, 1936; *Released:* April 12, 1936; *Executive Producer:* Robert North; *Producer:* Sid Rogell; *Director:* Albert S. Rogell; *Screenplay:* Fred Niblo, Jr., Earle Snell, Based on the Short Story by Diana Bourbon, with Contributions by Bruce Manning; *Photography:* Allen C. Siegler; *Additional Photography (airplane scenes):* Elmer Dyer; *Film Editor:* Otto Meyer; *Costumes:* Samuel Lange; *Sound Engineer:* Edward L. Bernds; *Sound Recordist:* George Cooper; *Assistant Director:* William Mull; *Casting of Chinese Extras:* Tom Gubbins (66 minutes)

Cast: Fay Wray (Joyce Reid), Ralph Bellamy (Dan Bailey), Thurston Hall (E. J. Reid), Edward Gargan (Andy Nelson), Roger Imhof (Capt. Murchison), Paul Guilfoyle (Dr. Wong), Tetsu Komai (Fang), Arthur Rankin (Blaney), Gene Morgan (Tex), Barnett Parker (Waters), Harold Goodwin (Reid's Pilot), William Gould (McLaughlin), Robert Strange (Kingston), Isabelle La Mal (Housekeeper), Charles Hamilton (Hardboiled Mechanic), Jehim Wong, Leo Abby, Luke Chan, George Chan, Richard Loo, Fraser Acosta, Val Duran, Edward Lee, Frank Fang,

Part II. Sound Films

Roaming Lady original release lobby card

Loo Loy (Chinese Men), Billy Arnold (Johnson), Bond Davis (Swanson), Jack Stewart (Detective)

Synopsis: Joyce Reid (FW), headstrong daughter of millionaire E. J. Reid, is in love with flight instructor Dan Bailey, who is employed by her father, and she publicly announces her engagement to Dan. E. J. Reid fires Dan when Joyce takes off in Reid's plane and performs dangerous aerial stunts, even though Dan had warned her not to do it. Knowing that Joyce is still in love with Dan, Reid sends Dan to China with his mechanic Andy, but Joyce follows. The trio is kidnapped by Dr. Wong, an Asian bandit. Joyce is held for ransom by Dr. Wong, but Dan and Andy escape with her. Joyce and Andy are pursued by Dr. Wong's men, but they are saved when Dan flies a plane overhead and bombs the gang. Finally safe, Joyce and Dan continue their romance, disregarding her father's objections.

Comments: Wray's first movie after returning to Hollywood from England found her in a standard madcap heiress role opposite Ralph Bellamy. The film, which featured more aviation adventure than comedy, was a slightly better-than-average Columbia effort. Said *Variety* in its review of May 6: "Miss Wray makes a gracious heroine despite the masculine outfit and tatters she is called on to wear during most of the feature."

They Met in a Taxi

Columbia, 1936; *Released:* September 1, 1936; *Producer:* Howard J. Green; *Director:* Alfred E. Green; *Screenplay:* Howard J. Green; *Story:* Octavus Roy Cohen; *Photography:* James Van Trees; *Art Director:* Stephen Gooson; *Film Editor:* Gene Milford; *Music:* Howard Jackson, Louis Silvers; *Music Director:* Morris Stoloff; *Sound Engineer:* George Cooper (69 minutes)

Cast: Chester Morris (Jimmy Donlin), Fay Wray (Mary Trenton), Raymond Walburn (Clifton), Lionel Stander (Fingers Garrison), Henry Mollison (Arnold Stewart), Kenneth Harlan (Andrews), Ann Merrill (Edna Fletcher), Ward Bond (Policeman at Stewart's Apartment), Frank Melton (Specks), James Flavin (Policeman), Alan Bridge (Detective), Rafael Storm (Count Postaki), Edward LeSaint

They Met in a Taxi

They Met in a Taxi: With Ward Bond (*far left*), Chester Morris (*facing Wray*) and Lionel Stander (*far right*)

(Justice of the Peace), Sam Ash (Elevator Man), Clarence L. Sherwood (Coffee John), Mary Lou Dix (Girl)

Synopsis: Socialite Edna Fletcher runs away from her own wedding and hides out in the apartment of taxi driver Jimmy Donlin. She then confesses that she is really Mary Trenton (FW), and reveals that she was modeling Edna's wedding gown when she was accused of stealing a pearl necklace. Panic-stricken, she fled, unaware that the missing necklace was hidden in the wedding gown.

Realizing that he will be implicated by the police since he has sheltered Mary, Jimmy talks a cab driver friend into surreptitiously returning the gown and necklace to Edna Fletcher's house. They then learn that the necklace was really stolen by Arnold Stewart, a financially desperate acquaintance of Edna's, and arrange for the police to find the evidence in Stewart's apartment. Mary, exonerated, then admits that she loves Jimmy.

Comments: The comedy-mystery had a stale plot, but was saved by the leads and a good supporting cast. It was filmed in less than four weeks during June and July of '36; the working title was *There Goes the Bride*. In its review of September 16, *Variety* said: "*They Met in a Taxi* is a modest little comedy that hasn't the heft for solo playing, but in the duals it will stand on its own. Fay Wray, as the girl, is okay except for a slight British accent she has developed. It's becoming for evening wear, but not when hanging around with a cab pilot."

It Happened in Hollywood

Columbia, 1937; *Released:* September 7, 1937; *Executive Producer:* William Perlberg; *Associate Producer:* Myles Connolly; *Director:* Harry Lachman; *Screenplay:* Ethel Hill, Harvey Fergusson, Samuel Fuller; Story by Myles Connolly; *Photography:* Joseph Walker; *Art Directors:* Stephen Gooson; *Film Editors:* Al Clark, Otto Meyer; *Gowns:* Kalloch; *Music Director:* Morris Stoloff; *Sound Engineer:* Lodge Cunningham; *Assistant Director:* Arthur Black (70 minutes)

Cast: Richard Dix (Tim Barry), Fay Wray (Gloria Gay), Victor Kilian (Slim), Franklin Pangborn (Mr. Forsythe), Charlie Arnt (Jed Reed), Granville Bates (Sam Bennett), William B. Davidson (Al Howard), Arthur Loft (Pete), Edgar Dearing (Stevens), James Donlan (Shorty), Billy Burrud (Billy), Zeffie Tilbury (Miss Gordon), Harold Goodwin (Buck), Charles Brinley (Pappy), Zeni Vatori (Joe Spogoli), Wade Boteler (Patrolman), Helen Brown, Mary Jane Temple (Nurses), Robert Chisholm (Englishman), Zita Moulton (Englishwoman), Tom Chatterton (Bank Manager), Byron Foulger (Chet), Sam McDaniel (Black Porter), Miki Morita (Japanese Gardener), Edward LeSaint (Doctor), Arthur Wanzer (Addison), D'Arcy

It Happened in Hollywood: Columbia Pictures studio portrait

Corrigan (Shakespearean Actor), Scotty Beckett, Delmar Watson, Bobby Watson, Tommy Bupp, Freddie Walburn, Wally Albright, Sammy McKim (Boys), Richard Terry, George Chesebro, Eddie Laughton (Gangsters), Don Brodie (Sound Man), Eddie Fetherston (Assistant Director), Beatrice Curtis (Script Girl), Edward Hearn (Cop), Lucille Lund (American Girl), Harry Strang (Joe Pratt), John Tyrrell (Burt), Cyril Ring (Cameraman), Frank Ellis (Gorman), George Billings (Tough Boy), Billy Wolfstone (Fat Boy), Charles Williams (Photographer), Alex Palasthy (Russian), Francis Sayles (Waiter), Bruce Sidney (Bank Manager), Philip Waldron (Clark Gable Double), Doc Dearborn (William Powell Double), Bob O'Keefe (James Cagney Double), Howard Bruce (Edward Arnold Double), Joan Beauchamp (Myrna Loy Double), Margaret Wormser (Loretta Young Double), John Bohm (John Barrymore Double), Arthur McLaglen (Victor McLaglen Double), James May (W. C. Fields Double), Eugene DeVerdi (Charles Chaplin Double), Charles Clark (Joe E. Brown Double), Frank Brown (Harold Lloyd Double), Virginia Rendell (Mae West Double), Carol Dietrich (Marlene Dietrich Double), Franky Farr (Eddie Cantor Double), Earl Haddon (Bing Crosby Double), Berna Mack (Claudette Colbert Double), Don Eddy (Dancing Fred Astaire Double), Lillian Tours (Dancing Ginger Rogers Double), Beatrice Coleman (Ginger Rogers Double), Betty Dietrich (Greta Garbo Double)

Synopsis: As the career of silent movie cowboy Tim Bart wanes with the arrival of the sound era, his co-star Gloria Gay (FW) grows more famous in the talkies. Tim had promised Billy, a disabled young fan, that he would introduce him to other Hollywood celebrities, and when he meets Billy again, he does not want to admit his own desperation and inability to keep his promise. Trying his best to fulfill Billy's wish, he throws a party for the boy, hiring doubles for the various Hollywood stars. Billy is injured when he tries to ride Tim's horse and falls off. Lacking money to provide medical care for Billy, Tim begs Gloria for a loan. She admits that she is broke, too, despite her apparent Hollywood success. Tim decides to rob a bank, but just as he is about to commit the robbery, real bank robbers appear on the scene, shooting a police officer. Tim draws his own gun, preventing the robbery and capturing the hoods. Hailed for his bravery, Tim sees his film career revived by the resulting publicity. His romance with Gloria is rekindled and the couple adopts Billy.

Comments: This Hollywood-on-Hollywood show business drama is somewhat reminiscent of *A Star Is Born* (released the same year). It's a pleasant little film, and one of Wray's best Columbia efforts. Shot on a five-week schedule (late March to early May '37), it had the working title *Once a Hero*.

Part II. Sound Films

Murder in Greenwich Village

Columbia, 1937; *Released:* October 16, 1937; *Executive Producer:* Irving Briskin; *Associate Producer:* Wallace MacDonald; *Director:* Albert S. Rogell; *Screenplay:* Michael L. Simmons; *Story:* Robert T. Shannon; *Photography:* Henry Freulich; *Art Directors:* Stephen Gooson, Lionel Banks; *Film Editor:* Dick Fantl; *Music;* George Parrish, Ben Oakland, Louis Silvers; *Music Director:* Morris Stoloff; *Gowns:* Robert Kalloch; *Sound Engineer:* Lambert Day. *Assistant Director:* Sam Nelson (66 minutes)

Cast: Richard Arlen (Steve Jackson), Fay Wray ("Lucky" Kay Cabot), Raymond Walburn (The Senator), Wyn Cahoon (Flo Melville), Scott Colton (Larry Foster), Thurston Hall (Charles Cabot), Marc Lawrence (Rusty Morgan), Gene Morgan (Henderson), Mary Russell (Antoinette/ "Angel Annie" MacGillicutty), George McKay (Officer), Leon Ames (Rodney Hunter), Barry Macollum (Murphy), Marjorie Reynolds (Molly Murphy), Howard Hickman (Mr. Sloan), Gordon DeMain (Capt. Bates), Eddie Fetherston, Dick Curtis (Campbell Cops), Bud Jamison, Bill Irving, Harry Hollingsworth, Jack Cheatham (Policemen), Edward Earle (Mr. Andrews), Nick Copeland, Vernon Dent (Ship's Officers), Al Herman (Signal Man), Wilson Benge (Butler), Edmund Cobb (City Cop), J. G. MacMahon (Steward), George Chesebro (Detective)

Synopsis: Heiress Kay Cabot (FW) climbs out the window of artist Phillip Morgan's studio after he makes improper advances, and is given shelter by another artist, Steve Jackson, who resides downstairs in the same building.

Learning that Morgan was murdered after Kay left his studio, Steve poses as Kay's fiancé to provide her with an alibi. Nevertheless, Kay is implicated in Morgan's killing and nearly arrested. Steve proves that the real murderer is Rodney Hunter, a friend of Kay's. Hunter is shot and killed by Rusty, Morgan's brother. The mystery of Morgan's killing solved, Kay realizes that she loves Steve.

Comments: Shot in less than three weeks (July–August '37, *Murder in Greenwich Village* is a less-than-successful mystery in the *Thin Man* vein — but it *does* open with an eye-catching scene of Wray climbing out of a building window and scampering down a fire escape in her underwear! It's all downhill from there. Its working title was *Park Avenue Dame*.

The Jury's Secret

Universal, 1938; *Released:* January 7, 1938; *Associate Producer:* Edmund Grainger, *Director:* Edward Sloman, *Screenplay:* Lester Cole, Newman Levy; *Story:* Lester

Cole; *Photography:* Milton Krasner; *Assistant Cameramen:* John Mehl, Robert Pierce, *Art Director:* Jack Otterson; *Associate Art Director:* Charles H. Clarke; *Film Editor:* Philip Cahn; *Music Director:* Charles Previn; *Wardrobe:* Frank Carr; *Ladies' Wardrobe:* Doris McCoig; *Sound:* Charles Carroll, Edwin Wetzel, Jack Rixey, Frank Gorbeck, J. Muchmore; *Hairstylist:* A. Armstrong; *Makeup:* Bill Ely; *Production Manager:* M. F. Murphy; *Gaffer:* John Brooks; *First Grip:* George Shuman; *Grip:* Frank Madigan; *Production Secretary:* Camille Collins; *Script Clerk:* Nagene Searle; *Still Photography:* Sherman Clark; *Assistant Propmen:* Les Hydeman, Ed Case; *Assistant Directors:* Fred Frank, Gil Valle, Jack Bernhard (62 minutes)

Cast: Kent Taylor (Walter Russell), Fay Wray (Linda Ware), Jane Darwell (Mrs. Sheldon), Nan Grey (Mary Morris), Larry Blake (William Sheldon), Fritz Leiber (John Morrow), Leonard Mudie (District Attorney), Samuel S. Hinds (Brandon Williams), Granville Bates (Judge Pendergast), Halliwell Hobbes (John, the Butler), Edward Broadley (Williams' Butler), William Davidson (Don Page), Billy Wayne (Baker), Robert Spencer (Jones), Ted Osborne (Reporter Thompson), Joe Cunningham, Drew Demarest, Frank O'Connor (Reporters), Harry C. Bradley (Jury Foreman), Bert Roach (Juror Hackenmier), Virginia Sale (Miss Montague, Juror), John "Skins" Miller (Juror Simms), Lillian Elliott (Mrs. Muller, Juror), Ferris Taylor (Attorney Appleby), Dick Rush (Bailiff), Art Yeoman, Jack Gardner, Ralph Brooks, Russ Powell, Charles Francis (Jurors), Tom Jackson (Jackson, Editor), Ben Lewis (Assistant Editor), Spencer Charters, Otto Hoffman (Old Men), Chester Clute (Secretary), Dick Elliott (Graves), Ben Taggart (Jenkins), Stanley G. Blystone (Mullen), William Gould (Sheriff), Robert Homans, Bruce Mitchell, William H. Royle (Cops), Ed Phillips (Brady), Hugh Huntley (Brennan), Elsa Christian (Dot Miller), Leonard Sues (Copy Boy), Ray Johnson, Edward Earl Kay, Lane Chandler (Men in Corridor), Heinie Conklin, Ernie Adams (Shabby Men), Betty Brown (Stylish Woman), Billy Engle (Waiter), Ed Brian (Messenger Boy), Broderick O'Farrell (Conductor), Frances Robinson (Dorothy Miller), William Lundigan (Announcer), Henry Hunter (Court Clerk), Harry Tenbrook, Charles Murphy, Betty Roche

Synopsis: Journalist Linda Ware (FW) investigates a series of devastating floods in Midland City, discovering that it is due to government neglect and the refusal of corrupt tycoon Brandon Williams to sponsor a disaster control bill.

When Walter Russell, a failed novelist who writes editorials for Williams' newspaper, decided to quit his job and leave town out of guilt, the duplicitous Williams tries to blackmail him into staying. Russell stabs and kills Williams.

Bill Sheldon, a spokesman for the townspeople, is blamed for the murder. With Sheldon on trial for his life, Linda Ware, a former girlfriend of Russell's, discovers that Russell murdered Williams. Appealing to Russell's better nature, she convinces him to admit his guilt.

Comments: This courtroom drama was filmed during November 1937 under various working titles including *More Than Love, Deadlocked* and *Deadlock*. *The Jury's Secret* was Wray's last film for Universal, the studio where she had started out as a teenager in the silent era. Some of the spectacular flood scenes, lifted from newsreels of actual disasters, were re-used by Universal in their popular serial *Flash Gordon's Trip to Mars*, starring Buster Crabbe, released shortly after this film. There the footage was used to depict the effects of a deadly ray aimed at the Earth by archvillain Ming the Merciless. Some filmgoers must have experienced a feeling of *deja vu*, since *The Jury's Secret* and episodes of *Flash Gordon's Trip To Mars* must have played many theaters together!

Smashing the Spy Ring

Columbia, 1938; *Released:* December 29, 1938; *Executive Producer:* Irving Briskin; *Producer:* Jack Fier; *Director:* Christy Cabanne; *Screenplay:* Arthur T. Horman, Dorrell McGowan, Stuart E. McGowan; *Story:* Dorrell McGowan, Stuart E. McGowan; *Photography:* Allen G. Siegler; *Art Director:* Lionel Banks; *Film Editor:* James Sweeney; *Music Director:* M. W. Stoloff; *Sound Engineer:* Edward L. Bernds; *Assistant Director:* Norman Deming (59 minutes)

Cast: Ralph Bellamy (John Baxter), Fay Wray (Eleanor Dunlap), Regis Toomey (Ted Hall), Walter Kingsford (Dr. L. B. Carter), Ann Doran (Madelon Martin), Warren Hull (Phil Dunlap), Forbes Murray (Col. Scully), Lorna Gray (Miss Loring), Paul Whitney (Mason), John Tyrrell (Johnson), May Wallace (Mrs. Baxter), Dick Curtis (Williams), Trevor Bardette (Jordan), Lee Prather (Major Nichols), Stanley Brown (Boy Vendor), Robert Fiske (Lieutenant General), Morgan Conway (Prof. Leonard), Bob Walker, Joe Palma, Philo McCullough (Workmen), Byron Foulger (Schuster/Quirk), Don Brodie (Casey), Harry Strang (Army Pilot), Henry Taylor, Eddie Fetherston (Cigar Store Proprietors), Mike Blair (Radio Commentator), Sam Ash (Doctor), Charles Moore (Lincoln), Beatrice Curtis (Anna), Reginald Simpson, Jack Egan (Reporters), Walter Merrill (Cameraman), Charles Hamilton (Fireman), George Magrill (Guard), Ed Laughton (Williams), Bud Geary (Taxi Driver), Rose Allen (Madelon's Maid), Cy Schindell (Richards), Bess Flowers (Mrs. Austin), Ralph Brooks (Operator)

Synopsis: Government agents John Baxter and Ted Hall capture Schuster, a spy, while they pose as employees at the Duncan Aircraft plant. They are reassigned to work with an associate, Philip Dunlap, in Washington, D. C., unaware that a second enemy spy, Steve Corbin, remains in the Duncan Aircraft plant. Dunlap is murdered as a result. Hall and Dunlap's sister Eleanor (FW) discover Dunlap's body, and together with Baxter resolve to track down the killers.

Eventually, Baxter and Eleanor, under assumed identities, trail the spy ring to a sanitarium run by Dr. L. B. Carter, exposing their activities. The spies, led by Dr. Carter, trap Baxter and Eleanor in the sanitarium lab, but they defend themselves by throwing bottles of acid at the spies until the police arrive and round up the enemy agents.

Comments: There must be a worse studio-produced film than *Smashing the Spy Ring*, but it certainly is difficult to think of one off-hand. Boring and uneventful, the best thing about the film is its title, which promises far more than the turgid movie attached to it is capable of delivering. This is easily Wray's worst film; the direction is so indifferent that she is not even allotted one close-up. Wray's career had lost vitality after her return from England and movie roles were growing scarce for the 31-year-old actress, who must have wondered how much worse things could get after landing in shabby material like this. Working titles for this film were *International Spy* and *Spy Ring*.

Navy Secrets

Monogram, 1939; *Released:* February 8, 1939; *Executive Producer:* Scott R. Dunlap; *Associate Producer:* William Lackey; *Director:* Howard Bretherton; *Screenplay:* Harvey Gates; Based on the Short Story "Shore Leave" by Steve Fisher); *Photography:* Harry Newman; *Film Editor:* Russell Schoengarth; *Sound:* Karl Zint; *Music:* Edward J. Kay; *Wardrobe:* Louis Brown; *Technical Director:* E. R. Hickson; *Production Manager:* Charles Bigelow; *Assistant Director:* W. B. Eason (60 minutes)

Cast: Fay Wray (Carol Matthews), Grant Withers (Steve Roberts/Fletcher), Dewey Robinson (Nick Cilatto), William von Brincken (Cronjer), Craig Reynolds (Jimmy), George Sorrell (Slavins), Andre Cheron (Joe Benje), Robert Frazer (Peter), Joseph Crehan (Daily), Duke York (Babe), Arthur Housman (Drunk), Joe Girard (Captain), I. Stanford Jolley

Synopsis: Naval Intelligence agent Carol Matthews (FW), operating incognito under the name Evans, investigates the theft of the Navy's new range finder by a spy ring.

Part II. Sound Films

Navy Secrets: With Grant Withers

Teaming up with Chief Petty Officer Steve Roberts, who is unaware that Carol is a government agent, they pursue the enemy agents. They fall in love in the course of their investigation. Steve is nearly murdered by the spies, but is rescued by Carol.

The police arrest the spy ring. Carol later meets Steve in a Naval Intelligence office, learning that he too is an undercover agent.

Comments: This tame espionage drama, quickly filmed by impoverished Monogram Pictures (the last refuge of the Bowery Boys and Bela Lugosi), was Wray's only film for the entire year of 1939. Although hardly a winner by any means, the film is at least a little better than her previous effort, *Smashing the Spy Ring*, and gave her billing over the main title. During production it was called *Navy Girl;* Anne Nagel was cast in Wray's part before filming began.

Wildcat Bus

RKO-Radio, 1940; *Released:* August 23, 1940; *Executive Producer:* Lee Marcus; *Producer:* Cliff Reid; *Director:* Frank Woodruff; *Story and Screenplay:* Lou Lusty;

Part II. Sound Films

Photography: Jack Mackenzie; *Special Effects:* Vernon L. Walker; *Art Director:* Van Nest Polglase; *Associate Art Director:* Lucius Croxton; *Film Editor:* George Crone; *Sound Engineer:* Frank Maher; *Music:* Roy Webb; *Stock Music:* Robert Russell Bennett, Arthur Lange, Nathaniel Shilkret; *Wardrobe:* Renie; *Assistant Director:* Kenneth Holmes (62 minutes)

Cast: Fay Wray (Ted Dawson), Charles Lang (Jerry Waters), Paul Guilfoyle (Donovan), Don Costello (Sid Casey), Paul McGrath (Stanley Regan), Joseph Sawyer (Burke), Roland Drew (Davis), Leona Roberts (Ma Talbott), Oscar O'Shea (Charles Dawson), Frank Shannon (Sweeney), Warren Ashe (Joe Miller), Chester Clute (Little Man), Max Wagner (Jackson/B. D.), Don Zelaya (Mexican), David Kerwin (Employment Clerk), Grace Hayle (Fat Woman), Henry Roquemore (Traveling Man), Henry Blair (Boy), Irene Charters (Girl), Norman Mayes (Porter), Ronnie Rondell (Bus Driver), Bud Fine (Foreman), Manart Kippen (Henry Walker), Landers Stevens (Doctor), Keye Luke (Tai), Martha Wentworth (Mrs. Waters), Minerva Urecal (Old Maid), Edgar Dearing (Cop), Ross Forrester

Wildcat Bus: With Paul Guilfoyle (*left*) and Charles Lang

(Driver), Bud Geary, George De Normand, Gil Perkins, Charles Regan, Mike Lally (Wildcat Drivers), Jack Gardner (Parking Lot Attendant), Frank Rapport (Hotel Clerk), Gohr Van Vleck (Cigar Clerk), Bob Perry (Hotel Porter), Jane Patten (Miss Waters)

Synopsis: Ted Dawson (FW) is the daughter of Federated Bus Line founder Charles Dawson and manages the company for her father. She is frustrated by an outbreak of suspicious accidents and mechanical failures undermining the business.

When down-and-out playboy Jerry Waters seeks employment at Federated, Ted turns him down, disliking him instantly. He lands a job with a rival wildcat taxi company. The company Waters goes to work for is managed by Sid Casey, who is conspiring with Joe Miller, general manager at Federated, to run Federated out of business.

Ted discovers this when she goes undercover on her own, posing as a passenger of the taxi service. Jerry discovers what Casey is up to and quits his job. Eventually, Ted learns that the saboteurs are led by the wife of Talbot, a corrupt former partner of her father's who had been imprisoned for embezzlement.

When she is confronted with her crimes, Mrs. Talbot falls down a flight of stairs to her death and the other gang members are arrested by the police, clearing the way for a developing romance between Ted and Jerry.

Comments: The best thing that can be said about *Wildcat Bus* is that Fay Wray at least looks good in it; the lovely actress is the film's *only* asset. Said *Variety* in its review of August 21: "Here is a mediocre actioner turned out on [a] low budget, that will get minimum total of bookings in the grind houses as a dual filler to consume running time on the bill. Nothing to recommend it anywhere along the line ... neither cast nor director can overcome the insipid material provided by the script, which apparently was okayed by the producer while looking out the window." *Wildcat Bus* was Wray's only film for 1940.

Adam Had Four Sons

Columbia, 1941; *Released:* February 18, 1941; *Producer:* Robert Sherwood; *Associate Producer:* Gordon S. Griffith; *Director:* Gregory Ratoff; *Screenplay:* William Hurlbut, Michael Blankfort, Based on the play *Legacy* by Charles Bonner; *Photography:* J. Peverell Marley; *Film Editor:* Francis D. Lyon; *Art Director:* Rudolph Sternad; *Music:* W. Franke Harling, Rudy Schrager; *Music Director:* C. Bakaleinikoff; *Makeup:* Robert J. Schiffer (108 minutes)

Top: Adam Had Four Sons: Columbia Pictures studio portrait; bottom: Adam Had Four Sons: Studio portrait.

Cast: Ingrid Bergman (Emillie Gallatin), Warner Baxter (Adam Stoddard), Susan Hayward (Hester), Fay Wray (Molly Stoddard), Richard Denning (Jack Stoddard as an Older Boy), Johnny Downs (David Stoddard as an Older Boy), Robert Shaw (Chris Stoddard as an Older Boy), Charles Lind (Phillip Stoddard as an Older Boy), Billy Ray (Jack Stoddard as a Younger Boy), Steven Muller (David Stoddard as a Younger Boy), Wallace Chadwell (Chris Stoddard as a Younger Boy), Bobby Walberg (Phillip Stoddard as a Younger Boy), Helen Westley (Cousin Phillipa), June Lockhart (Vance), Pietro Sosso (Otto), Gilbert Emery (Dr. Lane), Renie Riano (Photographer), Clarence Muse (Sam)

Synopsis: Businessman Adam Stoddard's wife Molly (FW) dies, and young housekeeper Emillie Gallatini is hired to care for his four sons as Stoddard's financial situation worsens.

As the boys mature into young men, Stoddard's personal fortunes improve, but the stability of his motherless family is disrupted by the machinations of Hester, who marries David, one of Adam's sons, and makes a play for David's brother Jack, who rejects her advances. Hester's true nature is eventually exposed, and Adam Stoddard realizes his love for Emillie.

Part II. Sound Films

Comments: In her second American film, Ingrid Bergman plays a housekeeper who cares for the sons of a businessman (Baxter) whose wife (Wray) has died. Wray appears in just a few scenes at the beginning of the film before her character's untimely demise. Despite a good story and solid acting from all involved, reviews for the picture were mixed, with many critics feeling that Bergman was definitely superior to her material.

Melody for Three

RKO-Radio, 1941; *Released:* March 28, 1941; *Producer:* William Stephens, Director Erle C. Kenton; *Screenplay:* Leo Loeb, Walter Ferris; *Photography:* John Alton; *Music:* C. Bakaleinikoff; *Film Editor:* Edward Mann; *Art Director:* Bernard Herzbrun; *Music Director:* C. Bakaleinikoff; *Assistant Director:* Glenn Cork (67 minutes)

Cast: Jean Hersholt (Dr. Paul Christian), Fay Wray (Mary Stanley), Walter Woolf King (Antoine Pirelle), Schuyler Standish (Billy Stanley), Patsy Lee Parsons (Nancy Higby), Irene Ryan (Mrs. Higby), Donnie Allen (Red Bates), Leon

Melody for Three: With Walter Woolf King

Tyler (Clarence), Andrew Tombes (Mickey), Irene Shirley (Mrs. Mitchell), Alexander Leftwich (Mr. Simpson), Toscha Seidel, Elvia Allman, Cliff Nazarro, Lois Austin

Synopsis: Kindly Dr. Christian attempts to reunite a divorced couple, music teacher Mary Stanley (FW), who is working as his nurse, and orchestra conductor Antoine Pirelle.

When Pirelle nearly dies in a plane crash, a distraught Mary is summoned by Dr. Christian to assist. Her romance with Pirelle is renewed and they reunite to enjoy the musical talents of their son, a gifted violinist.

Comments: This was a somewhat atypical entry in the popular *Dr. Christian* series, which starred character actor Jean Hersholt as the benign physician.

Not a Ladies' Man

Columbia, 1942; *Released:* May 14, 1942; *Producer:* Leon Barsha; *Director:* Lew Landers; *Screenplay:* Rian James, Based on the Story "Just Another Dame" by Robert Hyde; *Photography:* John Stumar; *Film Editor:* Mel Thorsen; *Art Director:* Lionel Banks; *Associate Art Director:* Perry Smith; *Music Director:* M. W. Stoloff; *Original Music:* John Leipold, Non-original Music: Ben Oakland (60 minutes)

Cast: Paul Kelly (Robert Bruce), Fay Wray (Pat Hunter), Douglas Croft (Bill Bruce), Ruth Lee (Jennie Purcell), Lawrence Dixon ("Pudge" Roberts), Marietta Canty (Lucy), Don Beddoe ("Professor" Johnson), Eileen O'Hearn (Margaret Vance), Jean Inness (Miss Murton), Louise Allbritton (Ethel Burbridge), William Wright (John Keen), Hal Price, Tristram Coffin, Jimmy Dakan, Dorothy Babb

Synopsis: Schoolteacher Pat Hunter (FW) visits Robert Bruce after she experiences difficulties in the classroom with Bruce's young son Bill. Learning that Bill's mother is gone, Pat gradually falls in love with Robert, but their romance is complicated by young Bill's misunderstanding. Gradually the difficulties are resolved as Bill finally realizes that Pat is the perfect wife for his father, as well as the mother he has always wanted and needed.

Comments: This innocuous family drama was Wray's last Hollywood film as a leading lady. The 35-year-old actress married screenwriter Robert Riskin the same year and retired; she would return to movies 11 years later in supporting roles.

Other things were in store for juvenile actor Douglas Croft; he would play Robin, the Boy Wonder, sidekick to comic book hero Batman, the following year in Columbia's 15-chapter serial *Batman*. *Not a Ladies' Man* was filmed under the source story's title, *Just Another Dame*.

Part III
1950s Feature Film Supporting Roles

Treasure of the Golden Condor

20th Century–Fox, 1953; *Released*: February 4, 1953; *Producer:* Jules Buck; *Director:* Delmar Daves; *Screenplay:* Delmar Daves, Based on the novel *Benjamin Blake* by Edison Marshall; *Photography (Technicolor):* Edward Cronjager; *Film Editor:* Robert Simpson; *Music:* Alfred Newman, Sol Kaplan; *Art Directors:* Lyle Wheeler, Albert Hogsett; *Costumes:* Dorothy Jenkins, Charles LeMaire (93 minutes)

Cast: Cornel Wilde (Jean-Paul), Constance Smith (Clara), Finlay Currie (MacDougal), Walter Hampden (Pierre), Anne Bancroft (Marie), George Macready (Marquis), Fay Wray (Marquise), Leo G. Carroll (Dondel), Konstantin Shayne (Curate), Louis Heminger (Indian Chief), Tudor Owen (Fontaine), Gil Donaldson (Count de Bayoux), Ken Herman (Francois), Bobby Blake (Stable Boy), Jerry Hunter (Jean-Paul at age 10), Wende Weil (Maria at age 8 1/2), Ray Beltram (Medicine Man), Edna Holland (Fontaine's Wife), Harry Cording (Breton), Crane Whitney (Ruffian), Donald Lawton (Dondel's Clerk), Robert Filmer (Bailiff), Camillo Guercio (Prosecutor), House Peters, Sr. (Magistrate), John Parrish (Turnkey), Alphonse Martell (Artist), May Wynn (Maid), Paul Bryar (Guard), Margaret Brayton

Synopsis: Jean-Paul, a dispossessed French aristocrat swindled out of his wealth by his treacherous uncle, travels to the jungles of Guatemala in search of treasure so that he can reclaim his estate. Although he succeeds in his quest, he is offended by the duplicity and corruption he finds among his peers after returning to France, and leaves to spend the rest of his days in Guatemala.

Comments: Wray returned to the film industry in supporting roles after her second husband, screenwriter Robert Riskin, was afflicted with and later died from a brain embolism. *Treasure of the Golden Condor*, a costume swashbuckler set in the jungles of Guatemala, was a remake of 20th's 1942 Tyrone Power vehicle *Son of Fury*, now with Wilde in Power's role. Wray was cast as villain George Macready's wife.

Small Town Girl

MGM, 1953 *Released*: April 10, 1953; *Producer:* Joe Pasternak; *Director:* Leslie Kardos; *Screenplay:* Dorothy Cooper, Dorothy Kingsley; Story by Dorothy Cooper; *Photography (Technicolor):* Joseph Ruttenberg; *Film Editor:* Albert Akst; *Music Director:* Andre Previn; *Art Directors:* Cedric Gibbons, Hans Peters; *Choreography:* Busby Berkeley; *Makeup:* William Tuttle (93 minutes)

Cast: Jane Powell (Cindy Kimbell), Farley Granger (Rick Belrow Livingston), Ann Miller (Lisa Belmount), S. Z. Sakall (Eric Schlemmer), Robert Keith (Judge Gordon Kimball), Bobby Van (Ludwig Schemmer), Billie Burke (Mrs. Livingston), Fay Wray (Mrs. Gordon Kimball), Chill Wills (Happy, the Jailer), Nat "King" Cole (Himself), Dean Miller (Mac), William Campbell (Ted), Philip Tonge (Hemmingway), Jonathan Cott (Jim, the Cop), Bobby Hyatt (Dennis), Rudy Lee (Jimmy), Beverly Wills (Deidre), Gloria Noble (Patsy), Jane Liddell (Betty), Nancy Valentine (Mary), Janet Stewart (Sandra), Pegi McIntire (Susie), Virginia Hall (Girl Friend), Marie Blake

Synopsis: Millionaire playboy Rick Belrow Livingston is arrested for speeding in a small town and is sentenced to 30 days in jail by Judge Gordon Kimbell. He eventually falls in love with the judge's daughter.

Comments: This MGM musical cast Wray in a small supporting role as the wife of Robert Keith's character. *Small Town Girl* bears no relation to an earlier 1936 MGM (non-musical) film of the same title starring Janet Gaynor. This 1953 movie features some enjoyable numbers by Ann Miller and Nat "King" Cole.

The Cobweb

MGM, 1955; *Released*: August 1955; *Producer:* John Houseman; *Associate Producer:* Jud Kinberg; *Director:* Vincente Minnelli; *Screenplay:* John Paxton; Based on the novel by William Gibson; *Photography (CinemaScope, Eastmancolor):* George Folsey; *Color Consultant:* Alvord Eiseman; *Film Editors:* Harold F. Kress, Conrad A. Nervig; *Art Directors:* Cedric Gibbons, E. Preston Ames; *Graphic Designer:* David Stone Martin; *Costumes:* Helen Rose; *Makeup:* William Tuttle; *Hair Stylist:* Sydney Guilaroff; *Sound:* Wesley C. Miller; *Assistant Director:* William Shanks (122 minutes)

Cast: Richard Widmark (Dr. Stewart McIver), Lauren Bacall (Meg Faversen Rinehart), Charles Boyer (Dr. Douglas N. Devanal), Gloria Grahame (Karen McIver), Lillian Gish (Victoria Inch), John Kerr (Steven W. Holte), Susan Strasberg (Sue Brent), Oscar Levant (Mr. Capp), Tommy Rettig (Mark), Paul Stewart (Dr. Otto Wolff), Jarma Lewis (Lois Demuth), Adele Jergens (Miss Cobb), Edgar Stehli (Mr. Holcomb), Sandy Descher (Rosemary), Bert Freed (Abe Irwin), Mabel Albertson (Regina Mitchell-Smythe), Fay Wray (Edna Devanal), Oliver Blake (Curly), Olive Carey (Mrs. O'Brien), Eve McVeagh (Shirley), Virginia Christine (Sally), Jan Arvan (Mr. Appleton), Ruth Clifford (Mrs. Jenkins), Myra Marsh (Miss Gavney), James Westerfield (James Petlee), Marjorie Bennett (Sadie), Stuart Holmes (Mr. Wictz)

Synopsis: Dr. Stewart McIver, the head of a psychiatric institute, finds himself burdened with the personal difficulties of his staff and their families, as well as the various neuroses of his patients.

Comments: A taut but generally depressing plot set in a psychiatric clinic, with a superlative cast and director. Wray was excellent in her supporting role as the troubled wife of Charles Boyer's character.

Queen Bee

Columbia, 1955; *Released:* November 7, 1955; *Producer:* Jerry Wald; *Director:* Ranald MacDougall; *Screenplay:* Ranald MacDougall; Based on the novel by Edna Lee; *Photography:* Charles Lang, Jr.; *Music:* George Duning; *Film Editor:* Viola Lawrence; *Music Director:* Morris Stoloff; *Sound Engineers:* John P. Livadary, Lambert E. Day; *Art Director:* Ross Bellah; *Costumes:* Jean Louis; *Makeup:* Clay Campbell; *Hair Stylist:* Helen Hunt; *Assistant Director:* Irving J. Moore (95 minutes)

Cast: Joan Crawford (Eva Phillips), Barry Sullivan (John Avery Phillips), Betsy Palmer (Carol Lee Phillips), John Ireland (Judson Prentiss), Lucy Marlow (Jennifer Stewart), William Leslie (Ty McKinnon), Fay Wray (Sue McKinnon), Katherine Anderson (Miss Breen), Tim Hovey (Ted), Linda Bennett (Trissa),

Willa Pearl Curtis (Miss George), Bill Walker (Sam), Olan Soule (Dr. Pearson), Bob McCord (Man), Juanita McCord (Maid)

Synopsis: Wealthy Eva Phillips, the devious wife of alcoholic mill owner John Avery Phillips, schemes to dominate those around her, manipulating their lives for her own personal amusement.

Comments: This Joan Crawford vehicle was Wray's first Columbia movie since *Not a Ladies' Man* in 1942.

Hell on Frisco Bay

Warner Bros., 1956; *Released:* January 28, 1956; *Producer:* George Bertholon; *Director:* Frank Tuttle; *Screenplay:* Sydney Boehm, Based on the *Collier's* magazine story "The Darkest Hour" by William P. McGivern; *Photography (CinemaScope, Warner Color):* John Seitz; *Music:* Max Steiner; *Film Editor:* Folmar Blangsted; *Art Director:* John Beckman; *Costumes:* Moss Mabry (98 minutes)

Cast: Alan Ladd (Steve Rollins), Edward G. Robinson (Victor Amato), Joanne Dru (Marcia Rollins), William Demarest (Dan Bianco), Paul Stewart (Joe Lye), Perry Lopez (Mario Amato), Fay Wray (Kay Stanley), Renata Vanni (Anna Amato), Nestor Paiva (Lou Franchetti), Stanley Adams (Hammy), Willis Bouchey (Lt. Neville), Peter Hanson (Detective Connors), Anthony Caruso (Sebastian Pasmonick), George J. Lewis (Father LaRocca), Tina Carver (Bessie), Rodney [Rod] Taylor (Brodie Evans), Peter Votrian (George Pasmonick), Jayne Mansfield (Blonde), Mae Marsh (Landlady)

Synopsis: Ex-con Steve Rollins, released from prison after serving time for a murder he did not commit, sets out to solve the crime and bring down the hood behind the killing, gangster Victor Amato.

Comments: A latter-day gangster melodrama, with Ladd going up against Edward G. Robinson, who essentially reprises his *Little Caesar* role as an older, middle-aged hood. A good cast keeps the film's tired plot interesting, culminating in an exciting speedboat chase in San Francisco. Wray looked attractive and was good in her supporting role as an aging former movie star, now gangster Paul Stewart's mistress. *Hell on Frisco Bay* was well-directed by Frank Tuttle, who had directed Alan Ladd in his star-making role in *This Gun for Hire* (Paramount, 1942). Rising sex symbol Jayne Mansfield and former silent screen star Mae Marsh were cast in small roles.

Part III. 1950s Feature Film Supporting Roles

Rock, Pretty Baby

Universal, 1957; Released: January 1957; *Producer:* Edmond Chevie; *Director:* Richard H. Bartlett; *Screenplay:* Herbert Margolis, William Raynor; *Photography:* George Robinson; *Music:* Henry Mancini; *Film Editor:* Frederick Y. Smith; *Music Director:* Joseph Gershenson; *Art Directors:* Alexanders Golitzen, Philip Barber; *Costumes:* Rosemary Odell; *Music and Lyrics:* Sonny Burke, Bill Carey, Bobby Troup, Rod McKuen, Phil Tuminello (89 minutes)

Cast: Sal Mineo (Angelo Barrato), John Saxon (Jimmy Daley), Luana Patten (Joan Wright), Edward C. Platt (Thomas Daley, Sr.), Fay Wray (Beth Daley), Rod McKuen ("Ox" Bentley), John Wilder ("Fingers" Porter), Alan Reed, Jr. ("Sax" Lewis), Douglas Fowley ("Pop" Wright), Bob Courtney ("Half-Note" Harris), Shelley Fabares (Twinkey Daley), Susan Volkmann (Carol Saunders), Carol Volkmann (Claire Saunders), April Kent (Kay Norton), Sue George (Lori Parker), Walter Reed (Mr. Reid), Glen Kramer (Bruce Carter), Johnny Grant (Himself), George "Foghorn" Winslow (Thomas Daley, Jr.), Geri Wilder (Girl), Jimmy Daley's Ding-A-Lings

Synopsis: Aspiring musician Jimmy Daley saves enough money to buy a guitar and join Angelo Barrato's band. The group puts on a show for local teenagers that ends up provoking a riot, with Jimmy and his friends paying for the resulting property damage.

Comments: A typical rock 'n' roll picture of the era, with a cast of overage "teenagers" (Mineo is the only actual teen in the cast); the older generation is represented by Edward C. Platt and Wray, as concerned parents.

Crime of Passion

United Artists, 1957; *Released:* February 1957; *Producer:* Herman Cohen; *Executive Producer:* Robert Goldstein; *Director:* Gerd Oswald; *Screenplay:* Jo Eisinger; *Photography:* Joseph LaShelle; *Music:* Paul Dunlap; *Film Editor:* Marjorie Fowler; *Art Director:* Leslie Thomas; *Set Design:* Morrie Hoffman; *Costumes:* Grace Houston; *Makeup:* Robert J. Schiffer; *Hair Stylist:* Shirley Madden; *Wardrobe:* Jack Masters; *Sound:* Francis J. Scheid; *Music Editor:* Jill Campbell; *Sound Effects Editor:* Verna Fields; *Props:* Joseph Thompson; *Script Supervisor:* Mary Gibsone; *Assistant Director:* Jack R. Berne (85 minutes)

Cast: Barbara Stanwyck (Kathy), Sterling Hayden (Doyle), Raymond Burr (Inspector Pope), Fay Wray (Alice Pope), Royal Dano (Alidos), Virginia Grey

(Sara), Dennis Cross (Detective Jules), Robert Griffin (Detective James), Jay Adler (Nalence), Malcolm Atterbury (Officer Spitz), John S. Launer (Chief of Police), Brad Trunbull (Detective Johns), Skipper McNally (Detective Jones), Robert Quarry (Reporter), Jean Howell (Mrs. Jules), Peg La Centra (Mrs. Jones), Nancy Reynolds (Mrs. Johns), Marjorie Owens (Mrs. Jones), John Conley (Delivery Boy), Stuart Whitman (Lab Technician), Eddie Kafafian, Geraldine Wall, Helen Jay, Madelon Erin, Sally Yarnell, Nan Dolan

Synopsis: Kathy, a hardboiled San Francisco newspaper columnist, marries Police Lt. Doyle, but cheats on him with his superior, Inspector Pope. When Pope throws her over, Kathy shoots and kills him, with Lt. Doyle eventually solving the crime and arresting his own wife.

Comments: A good cast (Stanwyck, Hayden and Burr) carries this melodramatic crime drama. Wray was cast in a supporting role as the wife of Burr's character.

Tammy and the Bachelor

Universal, 1957; *Released:* July 1957; *Producer:* Ross Hunter; *Director:* Joseph Pevney; *Screenplay:* Oscar Brodney; Based on the novel *Tammy Out of Time* by Cid Ricketts Sumner; *Photography (CinemaScope, Technicolor):* Arthur E. Arling; *Music:* Frank Skinner; *Film Editor:* Ted J. Kent; *Art Directors:* Richard H. Riedel, Bill Newberry; *Costumes:* Bill Thomas; *Special Effects:* Clifford Stine (89 minutes)

Cast: Debbie Reynolds (Tammy Tyree), Leslie Nielsen (Peter Brent), Walter Brennan (Grandpa), Mala Powers (Barbara), Sidney Blackmer (Prof. Brent), Mildred Natwick (Aunt Renie), Fay Wray (Mrs. Brent), Philip Ober (Alfred Bissle), Craig Hill (Ernie), Louise Beavers (Osia), April Kent (Tina)

Synopsis: Innocent country girl Tammy Tyree falls in love with Peter Brent, the scion of a wealthy plantation clan, winning over his snobbish family with her naive charm.

Comments: This comedy was the first in a series of three produced by Ross Hunter from the characters created by Cid Ricketts Sumner, and is the best of the lot. Debbie Reynolds is well-cast as a young backwoods girl whose positive outlook and sunny personality changes the lives of those around her. Fay Wray was cast as Leslie Nielsen's mother. The other two films in the series were *Tammy, Tell Me True* (1961) and *Tammy and the Doctor* (1963), both starring Sandra Dee as Tammy. A network TV series with Debbie Watson in the role followed.

Part III. 1950s Feature Film Supporting Roles

Dragstrip Riot

American-International, 1958; *Released:* March 1958; *Producer:* O. Dale Ireland; *Director:* David Bradley; *Screenplay:* George Hodgins, V. J. Rheims; *Story:* O. Dale Ireland, George Hodgins, V. J. Rheims; *Photography:* Gil Warrenton; *Music:* Nicholas Carras; *Film Editor:* John A. Bushelman (68 minutes)

Cast: Yvonne Lime (Janet Pearson), Gary Clarke (Rick Martin), Fay Wray (Mrs. Martin), Bob Turnbull (Bart Thorsen), Connie Stevens (Marge), Gabe DeLutri (Silva), Marcus Dyrector (Cliff), Ted Wedderspoon (Gramps), Barry Truex (Gordie), Marilyn Carroll (Rae), Maria Ryan (Helen), Steve Ihnat (Dutch), Tony Butula (Joe), Carolyn Mitchell (Betty), Joan Chandler (Lisa), Marc Thompson (Gary), Allan Carter (Mike)

Synopsis: Teenager Rick Martin joins a group of delinquents from wealthy families. The kids are soon involved in the death of a cyclist from a rival gang.

Comments: Wray was again cast as a concerned parent in this typical juvenile delinquent yarn. Connie Stevens, a petite and bubbly 19-year-old blonde in the cast, attained stardom on the ABC-TV network series *Hawaiian Eye* the following year.

Summer Love

Universal, 1958; *Released*: April 1958; *Producer:* William Grady; *Director:* Charles Haas; *Screenplay:* William Raynor, Herbert Margolis; *Photography:* Carl E. Guthrie, Clifford Stine; *Music:* Henry Mancini; *Film Editor:* Tony Martinelli; *Music Director:* Joseph Gershenson; *Art Direction:* Alexander Golitzen, Philip Barber (85 minutes)

Cast: John Saxon (Jim Daley), Molly Bee (Alice), Rod McKuen ("Ox" Bentley), Judi Meredith (Joan Wright), Jill St. John (Erica Landis), John Wilder (Mike Howard), George "Foghorn" Winslow (Thomas Daley III), Fay Wray (Beth Daley), Gordon Gebert (Tad Powers), Beverly Washburn (Jackie), Bob Courtney (Half-Note Harris), Troy Donahue (Sax Lewis), Hylton Socher ("Fingers" Porter), Marjorie Durant (Hilda), Walter Reed (Mr. Reid), Rock Murphy, Robert Bain, Plas Johnson, Jr., David Pell, Alvin Stoller, Ray Sherman, Mike Pacheco

Synopsis: Jimmy Daly, the leader of a rock 'n' roll group, gets a job at a summer camp and becomes romantically involved with two girls there as his band provides entertainment for the teenagers.

Comments: Rock, Pretty Baby had been successful enough to spawn this sequel,

Part III. 1950s Feature Film Supporting Roles

with most of the original cast returning in the same roles. Actor Troy Donahue, far down in the castlist, would later attain stardom in Warner Bros. TV shows like *SurfSide Six*. *Summer Love* was Wray's last theatrical film. Fay Wray also appeared as herself in the documentaries *Off the Menu: The Last Days of Chasens* (1997); *Frank Capra's American Dream* (1997); *Universal Horrors* (1998); *Broadway: The Golden Age, by the Legends Who Were There* (2003), directed by Rick McKay.

Appendix I
Appearances in Theatrical Shorts

Note: The length of each film is given in number of reels (each reel equals approximately 13 minutes of running time in the case of silent films, and 10 minutes at sound speed). The dates listed are the original Library of Congress copyright dates, except where noted.

Gasoline Love (1923); *Cast:* Fay Wray.

Thundering Landlords (Pathe, copyright April 10, 1925); *Producer:* Hal Roach; *Director:* James W. Horne; *Cast:* James Finlayson, Jackie Haynes, Glenn Tryon, Marjorie Whiteis, Fay Wray, Noah Young.

What Price Goofy? (Pathe, copyright May 18, 1925); *Producer:* Hal Roach; *Director:* Leo McCarey, two reels; *Cast:* Charley Chase (Charley), Katherine Grant (The Wife), Lucien Littlefield (Speck, the Butler), Noah Young (Omaha Oscar), Jane Sherman, Fay Wray.

Isn't Life Terrible? (Pathe, copyright May 29, 1925); *Producer:* Hal Roach; *Director:* Leo McCarey; *Photography:* Frank Jackman, Len Powers; *Assistant Director:* Lewis Foster; *Supervising Director:* F. Richard Jones; two reels. *Cast:* Charley Chase (Charley), Katherine Grant (The Wife), Oliver "Babe" Hardy (Remington), Lon Poff (Mr. Jolly), Leo Willis (A Mover), Fay Wray (Potential Customer), Sammy Brooks, Kathleen Collins, Mary Kornman, Jules Mendel, George Rowe.

Madame Sans Jane (Pathe, copyright June 25, 1925); *Director:* Hal Roach; *Cast:* James Finlayson, Glenn Tryon, Fay Wray, Lucien Littlefield.

Chasing the Chaser (Pathe, copyright July 6, 1925); *Producer:* Hal Roach; *Directors and Screenplay:* Stan Laurel, James Parrott; *Photography:* Art Lloyd; *Assistant*

Appendix I. Appearances in Theatrical Shorts

Director: Clarence Morehouse; *Supervising Director:* F. Richard Jones; two reels. *Cast:* James Finlayson (Gilroy), William Gillespie (Salesman), Sammy Brooks, Helen Gilmore, Jules Mendel, George Rowe, Marjorie Whitels, Fay Wray.

Moonlight and Noses (Pathe, copyright August 20, 1925); *Producer:* Hal Roach; *Director:* Stan Laurel; *Screenplay:* Carl Harbaugh, Stan Laurel; *Photography:* Harry W. Gerstad, R. H. Weller; *Assistant Directors:* Clarence Hennecke, Clarence Morehouse; two reels. *Cast:* Clyde Cook (A Burglar), Noah Young (A Burglar), James Finlayson (The Professor), Fay Wray (His Daughter), Tyler Brooke (Her Sweetheart), Marjorie Whitels, Helen Gilmore, William Gillespie, Jules Mendel.

No Father to Guide Him (Pathe, copyright August 25, 1925); *Producer:* Hal Roach; two reels. *Cast:* Charley Chase, Fay Wray.

Unfriendly Enemies (Pathe, copyright August 28, 1925); *Producer:* Hal Roach; *Director:* Stan Laurel; *Screenplay:* Stan Laurel, James Parrott; *Photography:* Art Lloyd; *Assistant Director:* Clarence Morehouse; *Supervising Director:* F. Richard Jones; two reels. *Cast:* James Finlayson (The Cameraman), George Rowe (His Assistant), Fay Wray (The Girl), Jules Mendel (Gen. Stonehead Balsam), Charlie Hall (First Soldier over the Top), Sammy Brooks, Helen Gilmore.

Your Own Back Yard (Pathe, copyright August 28, 1925) *Our Gang* series; *Producer:* Hal Roach; *Director:* Robert McGowan; *Story:* Hal Roach; *Titles:* H. M. Walker; *Film Editor:* Richard C. Currier; *Supervising Producer:* F. Richard Jones; two reels. *Cast:* Harry Bowen (Donor), Joe Cobb (Joe), Jackie Condon, Mickey Daniels, Johnny Downs, William Gillespie (Arguing Man), Fay Wray (Arguing Woman), Allen "Farina" Hoskins, Mary Kornman, Charles Oelze.

Should Sailors Marry? (Pathe, copyright December 30, 1925); *Producer:* Hal Roach; *Directors:* James Parrott, Jess Robbins; *Story:* Jess Robbins; *Titles:* H. M. Walker; *Photography:* Floyd Jackman; *Film Editors:* Richard C. Currier, Jess Robbins; *Assistant Director:* F. Richard Jones. *Cast:* Clyde Cook (Cyril D'Armond), Noah Young (The Ex-Husband), Fay Holderness (Verbina Singlefoot, the New wife), Martha Sleeper (Smyrna), Oliver Hardy (Doctor), William Gillespie (Train Passenger), Helen Gilmore (Train Passenger), Sammy Brooks, Kathleen Collins, Jules Mendel, Marjorie Whitels, Fay Wray.

One Wild Time (Universal, copyright March 2, 1926); *Director:* Vin Moore; *Story:* Robert McKenzie, W. C. Tuttle; two reels. *Cast:* Ben Corbett, Gilbert "Pee Wee" Holmes, Fay Wray, Dorothy Gulliver, Robert McKenzie

Don Key (A Son of Burro) (Pathe, copyright March 15, 1926); *Producer:* Hal Roach; *Directors:* Fred Guiol, James W. Horne, J. A. Howe; *Screenplay:* Hal Conklin, Carl Harbaugh, Grover Jones, Stan Laurel, Frank Terry, Hal Yates; *Photography:* Glen Carrier, Art Lloyd, Len Powers, Frank Young; *Film Editor:* George Nichols, Jr.; *Props:* Sherbourne Shields; *Assistant Director:* Jean Yarbrough; *Supervising Direc-*

Appendix I. Appearances in Theatrical Shorts

tor: F. Richard Jones; two reels. *Cast:* Max Davidson (Mr. Browning), Stuart Holmes (Aspiring Screenwriter), Spec O'Donnell (Office Boy), James Finlayson, Vivien Oakland, Tyler Brooke, Sammy Brooks, Frank Butler, Kathleen Collins, Dick Gilbert, William Gillespie, Helen Gilmore, Jackie Hanes, Lucien Littlefield (scenes deleted), Fred Malatesta, Jerry Mandy, Jules Mendel, Sue O'Neill, Laura Roessing, George Rowe (Barber), Yorke Sherwood, Martha Sleeper, Marjorie Whitels, Fay Wray, Noah Young

Don't Shoot (Universal, copyright July 15, 1926); *Mustang* Western Series; *Director:* William Wyler; *Story and Screenplay:* William Lester; two reels. *Cast:* Jack Mower, Fay Wray, Janet Gaynor (uncredited).

The Saddle Tramp (Universal, copyright September 13, 1926); *Mustang* Western Series; *Director:* Victor Nordlinger; *Screenplay:* Cecil Buris-Hill; two reels. *Cast:* Edmund Cobb, Fay Wray, Buck Connors, Palmer Morrison, Albert J. Smith.

WAMPAS Baby Stars of 1926 (1926); Six minutes. *Cast:* Joan Crawford, Mary Brian, Dolores Costello, Mary Astor, Vera Reynolds, Janet Gaynor, Sally O'Neil, Fay Wray, Joyce Compton, Marceline Day, Edna Marion, Sally Long (Themselves).

A Trip Through the Paramount Studios (1927); Nine minutes. *Cast:* Richard Arlen, Mary Astor, Clarence O. Badger, George Bancroft, Sally Blane, Clara Bow, Mary Brian, Betty Bronson, Chester Conklin, Dolores Costello, Shirley Dorman, Fanchon, W. C. Fields, Lloyd Hughes, Doris Kenyon, Fred Kohler, Blanche Le Clair, Mervyn LeRoy, Dorothy Mackaill, Arlette Marchal, Margo, Gene Morgan, Esther Robinson, Milton Sills, Fay Wray (Themselves).

The Stolen Jools (a.k.a. *The Slippery Pearls*) (Paramount, released April, 1931); *Producer:* Pat Casey; *Director:* William McGann; *Production Supervisor:* E. K. Nadel; two reels (sound). *Cast (in order of appearance):* Wallace Beery, Buster Keaton, Jack Hill, J. Farrell MacDonald, Edward G. Robinson, George E. Stone, Eddie Kane, Stan Laurel & Oliver Hardy, Norma Shearer, Polly Moran, Hedda Hopper, Our Gang, (Farina, Stymie, Chubby, Mary Ann Jackson, Shirley Dean Rickert, Echo, Wheezer, Pete the Pup), with Joan Crawford, William Haines, Dorothy Lee, Edmund Lowe, Victor McLaglen, El Brendel, Charlie Murray, Fifi D'Orsay, Winnie Lightner, Warner Baxter, George Sidney, Irene Dunne, Bert Wheeler & Robert Woolsey, Lowell Sherman, Richard Dix, Claudia Dell, Eugene Pallette, Stuart Erwin, Skeets Gallagher, Gary Cooper, Wynne Gibson, Buddy Rogers, Maurice Chevalier, Douglas Fairbanks, Jr., Loretta Young, Richard Barthelmess, Charles Butterworth, Bebe Daniels, Ben Lyon, Frank Fay, Barbara Stanwyck, Jack Oakie, Fay Wray, George "Gabby" Hayes, Little Billy, Joe E. Brown, Mitzi Green.

Comments: This special promotional short was made to raise funds for the relief work at the N. V. A. Tuberculosis Sanitarium at Saranac Lake, New York, which was later known as the Will Rogers Hospital for Respiratory Diseases. N. V. A., or National Variety Artists, was a company union of the Albee Theatre Chain.

Appendix I. Appearances in Theatrical Shorts

Hollywood on Parade #13 (Paramount, copyright July 28, 1933); *Producer:* Lewis Lewin, one reel (sound). *Cast:* Frankie Darro, Cary Grant, Leo Carrillo, Claudette Colbert, William Gaxton, Mary Boland, Anita Stewart, George Raft, Jean Harlow, Arline Judge, Fay Wray, Constance Cummings, Richard Dix, George Bancroft, Miriam Hopkins, Charlie Chaplin, Paulette Goddard (Themselves).

Appendix II
Television Appearances

Note: Dates given are original broadcast dates.

This Is Your Life episode honoring Pat O'Brien (June 10, 1953).

Pride of the Family (a.k.a. *The Paul Hartman Show*) (ABC, October 2, 1953 – September 24, 1954); Situation comedy series, 40 episodes, 30 minutes each; Produced by Revue Productions, *Distributor:* MCA Television; *Cast:* Paul Hartman (Albie Morrison), Fay Wray (Catherine Morrison), Natalie Wood (Ann Morrison), Bobby Hyatt (Junior).

Cavalcade of America episode "One Nation Indivisible" (December 22, 1953)

Damon Runyon Theatre episode *There's No Forever* (CBS, August 20, 1955)

Jane Wyman Presents the Fireside Theatre episode "Holiday in Autumn" (NBC, September 20, 1955)

Studio 57 episode *My Son Is Gone* (Syndicated, first broadcast October 2, 1955)

Screen Director's Playhouse episode "It's Always Sunday" (NBC, January 11, 1956)

The Twentieth Century-Fox Hour episode "In Times Like These" (February 22, 1956)

Studio 57 episode *Exit Laughing* (syndicated, first broadcast: April 1, 1956)

Jane Wyman Presents The Fireside Theatre episode "Killer's Pride" (NBC, January 29, 1957)

G. E. Theatre episode "The Iron Horse" (CBS, November 24, 1957)

Telephone Time episode "Alice's Wedding Gown" (syndicated, first broadcast: November 19, 1957)

Appendix II. Television Appearances

Kraft Television Theatre episode "Eddie" (NBC, January 22, 1958)

Alfred Hitchcock Presents episode "A Dip in the Pool" (CBS, September 14, 1958)

Perry Mason episode "The Case of the Prodigal Parent" (CBS, June 7, 1958)

Alfred Hitchcock Presents episode "The Morning After" (CBS, January 11, 1959)

The David Niven Show episode "The Promise" (NBC, May 5, 1959)

Playhouse 90 episode "The Second Happiest Day" (CBS, June 25, 1959)

Perry Mason episode "The Case of the Watery Witness" (CBS, October 10, 1959)

77 Sunset Strip episode "Who Killed Cock Robin?" (ABC, February 5, 1960)

Hawaiian Eye episode "The Bequest of Arthur Goodwin" (ABC, March 9, 1960)

The Islanders episode "Flight from Terror" (ABC, October 9, 1960)

The Real McCoys episode "Theatre in the Barn" (CBS, May 18, 1961)

G. E. Theatre episode "Money and the Minister" (CBS, November 26, 1961)

Wagon Train episode "The Cole Crawford Story" (NBC, April 11, 1962)

The Eleventh Hour episode "You're So Smart, Why Can't You Be Good?" (NBC, January 22, 1964)

Perry Mason episode "The Case of the Fatal Fetish" (CBS, March 4, 1965)

Gideon's Trumpet (CBS made-for-TV movie, April 30, 1980)

Index

Numbers in ***bold italics*** indicate photographs.

Abbott, George 49
ABC-TV 169
Abel, David 49
Acord, Art 2
Adam Had Four Sons (film) 159–***160***, 161
The Adventures of Robin Hood (film) 68
Affairs of Cellini (film) ***129–130***, 131–132
Alfred Hitchcock Presents (TV show) 176
Alias Bulldog Drummond see *Bulldog Jack*
Allan, Elizabeth 109
Allen, Gracie 132
American Film Institute 79
Ames, Leon see Waycoff, Leon
Angela Is 21 (play) 14
Ann Carver's Profession (film) 104–***105***, 106
Arbo, Manuel 49
Arlen, Richard 1, 39, 44, ***47***, ***48***
Armstrong, Robert 4, ***91***, ***95***, 102
Arsenic and Old Lace (play) 33
Arthur, Jean 44
Atwill, Lionel 65, ***76***, ***77***, ***81***, ***82***–83
Ayers, Lew 7

Baker, Rick 103
Bancroft, George ***38***
Banks, Leslie ***71***, ***72***
Barsky, Bud 17
Barthelmess, Richard 1
Batman (film serial) 116, 162
Baxter, Warner 161
Beery, Wallace 1, ***113***, 114, ***126***, 128
Behind the Make-Up (film) ***41***–42
Bellamy, Ralph 1, ***85***, 120, 148
Below the Sea (film) 83, ***84***, ***85***, ***86***
Bergman, Ingrid 161
Bernds, Edward L. 15, 124–125, 141
The Big Brain (film) 14, 107
Black Moon (film) 15, 122–***123***, 124–125
The Black Room (film) 125
Blood Sucker see *The Vampire Bat*
Bloodlust! (film) 75
The Blue Angel (film) 38
Borden, Olive 55
The Border Legion (1924 silent film) 46
The Border Legion (1930 film) ***45***–46
Boulting, Roy 75
Bow, Clara 114

The Bowery 112–***114***
The Bowery Boys 157
Boyer, Charles 165
Brian, Mary 44
Broadway: The Golden Age, By the Legends Who Were There (documentary) 170
Brody, Steve 114
Brown Danube (play) 14
Buchanan, Jack 142
A Bucket of Blood (film) 83
Bulldog Jack (film) ***145***–146
Burgess, Dorothy 128
Burr, Raymond 168
Buzzell, Eddie 106

C&C 107
Cabot, Bruce ***91***, ***96***, ***97***, 101, 102
Cagney, James 111
Cameron, James 14
Capone, Al 57
Capra, Frank 1, 56, 106
Captain Thunder (film) 49–***50***, 51, 128
Carson, Jack 111
Casablanca (film) 68, 107
Cavalcade of America (TV show) 175
Chamber of Horrors (film) 83
Chang (film) 99
Chase, Charley 1

177

Index

Chasing the Chaser (film short) 171–172
Cheating Cheaters (film) 134–135
The Chicago Tribune (newspaper) 57
Citizen Kane (film) 61
C.K.Y. Film Corp. 135
The Clairvoyant (film) *144*–145
The Coast Patrol (film) 1, 17–*19*
The Cobweb (film) 164–166
Cohn, Harry 56, 106
Colbert, Claudette 7
Cole, Nat "King" 164
Colman, Ronald *59*, *60*, 61
Columbia Pictures 4, 14, 15, 56, 116, 125, 139, 141, 148, 162, 166
Come Out of the Pantry (film) 141–*142*
Compson, Betty 135
Connell, Richard 74, 75
Conquering Horde (film) *51*–*52*, 53
Conway, Jack 1, 128
Cooper, Gary 1, *23*, *24*, 44, *110*, *111*
Cooper, Merian C. 4, 37, 99, 100, 101, 103
The Countess of Monte Cristo (film) 14, 120, *121*, 122
Crabbe, Larry "Buster" 74, 155
Crawford, Joan 166
Crime Commission of Washington, D.C. 139
Crime of Passion (film) 167–168
Croft, Douglas 162
Curtiz, Michael 1, 68, 70, 81, 83

Damon Runyon Theatre (TV show) 175
The David Niven Show (TV show) 176
Deadlock see *The Jury's Secret*
Deadlocked see *The Jury's Secret*
Dee, Sandra 168
de Havilland, Olivia 111

Delgado, Marcel 99
de Mille, Katherine 128
de Toth, Andre 83
El Dios del Mar see *The Sea God*
Dirigible (film) 4, 15, 55–67
Dr. Christian (film series) 162
Doctor X (film) 1, 4, 9, 11, 64–*65*, *66*, *67*, *68*, *69*, 81, 128
Don Key (A Son of Burro) (film short) 172–173
Donahue, Troy 170
Don't Shoot (film short) 173
Dore, Gustave 99
Dracula (film) 69, 77, 119
Dragstrip Riot (film) 169
Dwan, Allan 135

Eburne, Maude *78*
Edeson, Arthur 107
Empire State Building 15, 99, 103
The Evil Mind see *The Clairvoyant*

Farrell, Glenda *79*, 81, 82
Fields, W.C. 37
Film Daily (periodical) 128
The Finger Points (film) 57
The First Kiss (film) 25–*26*
First National 99
Fischbeck, Harry 25
Flash Gordon (film serials) 74
Flash Gordon's Trip to Mars (film serial) 155
Fonda, Henry 14
Forced to Sin see *The Vampire Bat*
Fort, Garrett 141
Foster, Preston *66*
Foster, Susanna 14
The Four Feathers (1929 film) 4, 35–*36*, 37, 99
The Four Feathers (1939 film) 37
Fox Film Corp. 109
Frank Capra's American Dream (documentary) 170
Frankenstein (film) 69, 70, 107
Frankenstein Meets the Wolf Man (film) 125
Freund, Karl 1, 14, 119, 122

Frolich, Gustav 119
Frye, Dwight 77
Fuller, Frances *111*

Gable, Clark 57, 114, 134
Game of Death (film) 75
Garbo, Greta 25
Gasoline Love (film short) 1, 171
Gaynor, Janet 19, 164
G. E. Theatre (TV show) 175, 176
Gibson, Hoot 2
Gideon's Trumpet (made-for-TV movie) 14, 176
Glennon, Bert 25
Golden Wings (play) 14
Goldstone, Phil 76
Goldwyn, Samuel 61
Gone with the Wind (film) 128
Die Graefin von Monte Cristo see *The Countess of Monte Cristo*
Grass (film) 99
Graves, Ralph 56
Greed (film) 27
Greer, Jane 75
Griffith, Andy 75
Guilfoyle, Paul *158*
Guillermin, John 102

Hagen, James 110
Hall, James 44
Hammer Films 70
Harlan, Kenneth 135
Harryhausen, Ray 99, 102
Hartl, Karl 122
Hawaiian Eye (TV show) 169, 176
Hawks, Howard 128
Hayden, Sterling 168
Hays Office 132
Hayworth, Rita 111
Hecht, Ben 61
Hell on Frisco Bay (film) 166
Hell's Angels (film) 56
Hersholt, Jean 162
Hillyer, Lambert 116, 119
Hollywood on Parade #13 (film short) 174
Holmes, Phillip *40*
Holt, Jack 1, 53, 116, 123, 135

Index

The Honeymoon (film) 4, 28, 34
Hope, Bob 37
Hopkins, Miriam 134
House of Wax (film) 83
Houseman, John 14
Hoxie, Jack 2
Hughes, Howard 14, 61

International Spy see *Smashing the Spy Ring*
Isn't Life Terrible? (film short) 171
It Happened in Hollywood (film) **151**–152

Jackson, Peter 103
Jane Wyman Presents the Fireside Theatre (TV show) 175
Jannings, Emil 1, 25, **26**
Johnson, Noble **71**
Jory, Victor 139, 141
The Jury's Secret (film) 153–155
Just Another Dame see *Not a Ladies' Man*

K.B.S. Productions 107
Karloff, Boris 19, 26, 61, 68, 119
Kelly, Patsy 122
King, Walter Woolf **161**
King Kong (1933 film) 87–98, 1, 4, 5, 7, 10–11, 37, 69, 74, 87, **88–89, 90–91, 92–93, 94–95, 96–97**, 98–102
King Kong (1976 film) 102
King Kong (2005 film) 103
King Kong Escapes (film) 102
King Kong vs. Godzilla (film) 102
Kirk, Phyllis 83
Kraft Television Theatre (TV show) 176
Krasna, Norman 134

Ladd, Alan 166
Laemmle, Carl 1–2, 20, 32
Laemmle, Edward 135
Lake Arrowhead (Calif.) 134

Land Rush see *Not Exactly Gentlemen*
Lang, Charles **158**
Lange, Jessica 102
Laughton, Charles 132
Laurel, Stan 1
The Lawyer's Secret (film) 58
Lazy Lightning (film) 20
Lee, Lila 128
Lee, Rowland V. 26
Legion of the Condemned (film) 4, 22, **23–24**, 39
Lewis, Sinclair 14
Lingle, Jake 57
Lippman, Irving 124
Little Caesar (film) 166
Loco Luck (film) 20–21
Loder, John 75
Long, Audrey 75
The Lost World (film) 99
Loy, Myrna 128
Lugosi, Bela 119, 157

MacArthur, Charles 61
MacReady, George 164
Madame Sans Jane (film short) 171
Madame Spy (film) 14, **116–119**, 122
The Making of King Kong (book) 15
The Maltese Falcon (film) 107
Man in the Saddle (film) 17–19
Manhattan Melodrama (film) 134
Mansfield, Jayne 166
March, Fredric 1, **130**
Marcin, Max 135
Maris, Mona 128
Marsh Mae 166
The Marx Bros. 37
Mason, A.E.W. 37
Master of Men (film) 115
McCrea, Joel 1, **71, 72, 73**, 74
McDonald, Kenneth 17
McLaglen, Victor **54**
Melody for Three (film) **161**–162
Men of Steel see *Master of Men*
Metropolis (film) 119
Meyer, Johannes 119
MGM 13, 56, 109, 128, 134

Mighty Joe Young (film) 102
Miller, Ann 164
Mills of the Gods (film) 15, **140**–141
Milner, Victor 25
Mineo, Sal 167
Mr. Big (play) 14
Mr. Ed (TV show) 64
Monogram Pictures 14, 157
Monroe, Marilyn 100
Moonlight and Noses (film short) 172
More Than Love see *The Jury's Secret*
Moreno, Francisco 49
Moreno, Paco 49
Moreno, Rosita 49
Morgan, Dennis 111
Morgan, Frank **130, 131**, 132
Morgan, Ira 77
Morris, Chester **150**
The Most Dangerous Game (film) 1, 4, 9, 37, **70, 71, 72, 73**, 74–75
Motion Picture Herald (periodical) 74
The Mummy (film) 61, 119
Murder in Greenwich Village (film) 153
Murders in the Rue Morgue (film) 119
Myers, Carmel 128
Mystery of the Wax Museum (film) 1, 4, 9, 11, 68, 78–**79, 80–81**, 82–83

Nagel, Anne 157
Navy Girl see *Navy Secrets*
Navy Secrets (film) 156–**157**
Neill, Roy William 1, 15, 124–125, 141
Nielsen, Leslie 168
Nikki (play) 14
No Father to Guide Him (film short) 172
North of 36 (film) 53
Not a Ladies' Man (film) 14, 162, 166
Not Exactly Gentlemen (film) 53–**54**, 55

O'Brien, George 55
O'Brien, Willis H. 99, 102

Index

O'Connor, Donald 14
Odets, Clifford 14
Off the Menu: The Last Days of Chasens (documentary) 170
Offeman, Emil 30, 32
On the Other Hand (book) 15, 109
Once a Hero see *It Happened in Hollywood*
Once to Every Woman (film) 119–**120**
A One Man Game (film) 21
One Sunday Afternoon (1933 film) 109–**110**, 111, 115
One Sunday Afternoon (1949 film) 111
One Wild Time (film short) 172

Paige, Janis 111
Pallette, Eugene **108**
Paramount on Parade (film) 42–**43**, 44
Paramount Pictures 4, 5, 23, 37, 38, 39, 42, 46, 53, 58, 110
Park Avenue Dame see *Murder in Greenwich Village*
The Paul Hartman Show see *Pride of the Family*
Perry Mason (TV show) 176
Pichel, Irving 4
Platt, Edward C. 167
Playhouse 90 (TV show) 176
Pogany, Willy 61
Pointed Heels (film) 39–**40**, 41
Powell, William 1, 39, 42
Power, Tyrone 164
Powers, P.A. "Pat" 27
Price, Vincent 83
Pride of the Family (TV show) 175
Professional Women see *Ann Carver's Profession*

Queen Bee (film) 165–166

Raft, George **113**, 114
Rains, Claude 1, **144**
Rathbone, Basil 124
Raymond, Gene **105**

Reicher, Frank **91**
Reynolds, Debbie 168
The Richest Girl in the World (film) 132–**133**, 134
Riskin, Robert 105, 162
Riskin, Robert, Jr. 14
Riskin, Susan 14
Riskin, Victoria 14
RKO-Radio 14, 99, 107, 134
Roach, Hal 1, 122
Roaming Lady (film) 147–**148**
Robinson, Edward G. 166
Rock, Pretty Baby (film) 167
Rogers, Ginger **7**
Romero, Cesar 135
Rosener, George **67**
Rothenberg, Dr. Sanford F. 14
Rules for Wives see *Ann Carver's Profession*
Run for the Sun (film) 75

The Saddle Tramp (film short) 173
Saunders, John Monk 4, 14, 23, 57
Scarface (film) 61
Schoedsack, Ernest B. 4, 37, **92**, 99, 101
Screen Director's Playhouse (TV show) 175
The Sea God (film) 46, **47**, **48**, 49
Selznick, David O. 128
The Seven Year Itch (film) 100
Seventy-Seven Sunset Strip (TV show) 176
Shanghai Madness (film) 107–**108**
Sherlock Holmes (film series) 124–125
Should Sailors Marry? (film short) 172
Skull Island see *The Most Dangerous Game*
Small Town Girl (film) 164
Smashing the Spy Ring (film) 155–156, 157
Society Doctor (film) 128
Son of Frankenstein (film) 26
Son of Fury (film) 164
The Son of Kong (film) 102

Spurs and Saddles (film) 22
Spy Ring see *Smashing the Spy Ring*
Stampede see *The Conquering Horde*
Stander, Lionel **150**
Stanwyck, Barbara 168
A Star Is Born (film) 152
Star Wars (film) 99
Steiner, Max 7, 99, 103
Stevens, Connie 169
Stewart, Paul 166
Stiller, Mauritz 1, 25, **26**
The Stolen Jools (film short) 173
Stout, Archie 49
Stowaway (film) 61–**62**, **63–64**
The Strawberry Blonde (film) 111
Street of Sin (film) **25**–26, 39
Stuart, Gloria 14
Studio 57 (TV show) 175
Summer Love (film) 169–170
Sumner, Cid Ricketts 168
Sunset Blvd. (film) 34
Surfside Six (TV show) 170
Susa, Charlotte 119
Swanson, Gloria 34

Tammy and the Bachelor (film) 168
Tammy and the Doctor (film) 168
Tammy Tell Me True (film) 168
Tampico see *The Woman I Stole*
Telephone Time (TV show) 175
The Terror (play) 69
The Texan (film) ***frontispiece***, 44–45
There Goes the Bride see *They Met in a Taxi*
They Met in a Taxi (film) **149**–151
The Thin Man (film) 39
The Thin Man (film series) 153
This Gun for Hire (film) 166
This Is the Life (film) 14

Index

This Is Your Life (TV show) 175
Three Bad Men see *Not Exactly Gentlemen*
Three Rogues see *Not Exactly Gentlemen*
Three Rough Diamonds see *Not Exactly Gentlemen*
Thunderbolt (film) 4, 37–*38*, 39
Thundering Landlords (film short) 171
Titanic (film) 14
Tobis Films 119
Toland, Greg 61
Tower of London (film) 26
Track of the Vampire (film) 83
Tracy, Lee *66*, *67*, 128
Tracy, Spencer 1, *108*, 109, 134
Treasure of the Golden Condor (film) 163, 164
Trevor, Claire 109
Tricked see *Stowaway*
A Trip Through the Paramount Studios (film short) 173
Turner, George 15
Turner, Ted 79
Tuttle, Frank 166
Twentieth Century–Fox 109, 114, 115, 164
The Twentieth Century–Fox Hour (TV show) 175
Twentieth Century Pictures 114, 134

UCLA 81
UFA Studios 122
Unfriendly Enemies (film short) 172
The Unholy Garden (film) 58–*59*, *60*–61
United Artists 79
Universal Horrors (documentary) 170
Universal Pictures 2, 14, 20, 21, 22, 26, 28, 32 37, 61, 69, 70, 76, 119, 155
Unter Falscher Flagge see *Madame Spy*

The Vampire Bat (film) 1, 9–10, 75–*76*
Variety (periodical) 17, 20, 21, 26, 34, 38, 39, 49, 56, 69, 128, 151, 159
Varnac, Denise 33
Venturini, Edward D. 49
Villa, Pancho 128
Viva Villa! (film) 13, *125*–*126*, 127–128
von Sternberg, Joseph 1, 4, 38
von Stroheim, Erich 1, 4, 22, 27–28, *29*, 32–34

Walker, Joseph 84
The Walking Dead (film) 68
Walsh, Raoul 111, 114
Wampas Baby Stars of 1926 (film short) 173
Warner Bros. (Warner Bros.–First National) 4, 39, 83, 111, 114, 116
Watson, Debbie 168
Wax Museum see *Mystery of the Wax Museum*
Waycoff, Leon 64
Wayne, John 49, 56
Wead, Commander Frank Wilber 56
The Wedding March (film) *2*, 14, 22–*29*, *30*–*31*, 32–34
Wellman, William 1
West, Mae 37
Whale, James 70
What Price Goofy? (film short) 171
When Knights Were Bold (film) *146*–147
White Lies (film) 137–*138*, 139
Widmark, Richard 75
Wild Horse Stampede (film) 19
Wildcat Bus (film) 157, *158*, 159
Wilder, Billy 37
Willat, Irvin 53
Wings (film) 4
The Wings of Eagles (film) 56
Wise, Robert 75
Withers, Grant *157*
The Woman I Stole (film) 103–104
Woman in the Dark (film) 135–*136*, 137
Wray, Fay (biography) 1–15
Wray, John *67*
Wyler, William 20, 33

Young, Alan 64
Young, Clara Kimball 135
Your Own Back Yard (film short) 172

Zanuck, Darryl F. 113, 132

www.ingramcontent.com/pod-product-compliance
Ingram Content Group UK Ltd.
Pitfield, Milton Keynes, MK11 3LW, UK
UKHW050523150426
5217IPUK00026B/1773